HERE'S THE
PLAN.

HERE'S THE
PLAN.

Your Practical,
Tactical Guide to
Advancing Your Career
During Pregnancy
and Parenthood

ALLYSON DOWNEY

SEAL PRESS

Library of Congress Cataloging-in-Publication Data
Names: Downey, Allyson, author.
Title: Here's the plan: your practical, tactical guide to advancing your career during pregnancy and parenthood / Allyson Downey
Description: Berkeley, California: Seal Press, [2015]
Identifiers: LCCN 2015040214 | ISBN 9781580056182
Subjects: LCSH: Working mothers. | Career development. | Work and family. | Work-life balance. | Vocational guidance for women.
Classification: LCC HQ759.48 .D695 2015 | DDC 306.3/6—dc23
LC record available at http://lccn.loc.gov/2015040214

Published by
Seal Press
A Member of the Perseus Books Group
1700 Fourth Street
Berkeley, California
Sealpress.com

Cover design by Kara Davison, Faceout Studio
Interior design by Domini Dragoone

Printed in the United States of America
Distributed by Publishers Group West

CONTENTS

AUTHOR'S NOTE

When I conducted interviews and collected stories for this book, I wanted women to speak freely. I told them they didn't need to censor themselves or worry that they could inadvertently say something that could damage their careers.

Unless someone gave me explicit permission to use her name in connection with a specific quote or story, I've shielded her identity and just noted her role and a company name or industry.

INTRODUCTION

A couple of years after I finished business school, there was a point at which all of my friends were pregnant. It was like a chain reaction via email: "I'm having a baby in January!" "Me too!" "I'm due in November!" Though it felt like a bizarre coincidence, it shouldn't have. Having established a little professional stability, it made sense that it was "time" to start families. But this sudden sense of community was particularly striking, because before this email exchange, I—like many newly pregnant women—had felt terribly alone. It was an epiphany to know that I wasn't. (It doesn't help that we're expected, even encouraged, to keep our pregnancies secret until the end of the first trimester.)

No one talks about pregnancy in professional terms before you get pregnant. You might have a colleague who has taken maternity leave, or you might have done some digging during your interview process to find out what the policies were. But there's no coursework or formal training in how to keep your career on track when you have a baby. My friend Margo called it "the missing class" in our MBA educations. "It would have been a lot more practical for me," she said, "than the price elasticity of demand and microeconomic theory. Should we send a note to the dean?"

Many women, for instance, are astonished to find that they aren't entitled to any paid parental leave after the birth of a child; to get any paid time off they need to cobble together accrued vacation time or sick leave. To really give us the advance notice we need to save enough funds, this information should be shared in high school—never mind in college or graduate school.

Another astonishing thing: how deeply ingrained and pervasive bias can be. Many women encounter bias from other women, from colleagues with young families, from self-proclaimed feminists, and from companies that trumpet their commitment to supporting women. There's this overwhelming sense that if you're at the "right" company, in the right job with the right manager, you'll be okay—but even in the very best of circumstances, you may find yourself derailed. I did.

In 2010, I graduated from Columbia Business School with a plum job lined up on Wall Street. I say "plum" because I consciously chose it; I had a strong sense of what I wanted, and I researched it carefully before deciding. For starters, a commission-driven business-development role appealed to me: generate X revenue for the firm, get paid Y dollars. Clear, quantifiable metrics of success seemed perfectly aligned with having a family: if you were meeting or exceeding your goals, who could question your commitment? And since so much of the job was about meeting with clients, I could bend those meetings around my schedule. The concept of forced face time (the act of physically being present at the office, to signal that you're working hard) was less relevant in this position, so ducking out for a pediatrician visit or coming in after school drop-off felt very feasible.

One particular firm courted me aggressively, and whenever I sat down to meet with a woman, I asked her about balance and family. I raised those questions candidly, whether it was an off-the-record informational session or a formal interview, and I think I received candid answers.

At the time, I talked to every woman I could. Pretty soon after I started my job, I realized I had in fact talked to *all* of them—and the private banking division of this global investment bank had only a handful of nonadministrative women. I should have seen that red flag early on: on the day when I received my job offer, two managing directors took me to lunch. After we made all the requisite small talk, they asked me to join the firm, and I asked offhandedly what percentage of the division was female. But while I had requested a number, they answered me in names. "Well, there's ____, ____, ____ in New York and ____ in Boston. We've got ____ in San Francisco, and ____ in Chicago." Now, I don't think it was an exhaustive list, but they were doing the mental equivalent of counting their (nonsecretarial) female employees on their fingers.

I saw this overwhelmingly male culture as an exciting challenge. I was sure I had more mettle than the women who'd come before me; I was more tenacious and assertive. I believed that—if I wanted it badly enough, if I worked hard enough—my gender need have nothing to do with my ability to succeed on Wall Street.

And I was right—for a while. The same calculated, meticulous, incessant follow-through that had served me well in previous jobs was starting to work for me in this role, too, and the firm noticed. In one of our quarterly check-ins, the managing director who ran the New York office—essentially my boss's boss—told me that, in a field with a notoriously high attrition rate, he believed I was their best hope for success out of our incoming MBA class. Soon after, I announced my pregnancy, and I told him (and everyone else who would listen) I planned to take only six weeks of maternity leave. I was up-front and emphatic about an abbreviated leave because I wanted to signal how committed I was to the job and show my managing director that his confidence in me was justified.

But a couple of weeks later my doctor, concerned about preterm labor, told me, "I want you off your feet. You should be working from home 75 percent of the time." From that appointment I went straight to my office, having emailed my direct manager en route. I packed up my laptop, pulled together documents for face-to-face meetings, got a network-access encryption key from IT, and left. I was scared, but not about my job: I could make phone calls and send emails from anywhere. This wasn't going to slow me down.

The first problems I encountered manifested as just red tape details. My encryption key wasn't working, but IT couldn't get to it right away, and they didn't know how to install the phone software I'd need to make calls from home in compliance with company policy. But then, because it looked like I was progressing toward labor, I had a few emergency trips to the hospital. I was 23 weeks pregnant; if you deliver at that gestational stage, there's only a 10 percent survival rate. "If you can get to 24 weeks," my doctor said, "it's 50 percent."

I fired off an email to my firm, sending it to both my boss and my HR contact. I explained that I had to be entirely off my feet, but emphasized that I would still like to work from home. I asked to set up some time to discuss logistics.

No response. Voicemails I sent to the same effect also got no response. I emailed the managing director who ran the New York office. Silence.

I did this every day for two weeks. I also started Googling "employment protection during pregnancy" and "how do I find an employment attorney." Wracked with anxiety, not just about my baby but now also about my job, I asked my doctor what to do. Was I about to lose everything in one fell swoop? "Copy me on your emails to them," she said. "Ask them what additional documentation they need."

It worked: I got a call from Human Resources. The HR contact told me simply, "On Monday, you should call our insurance provider to initiate your disability leave." She didn't present it as a choice or offer me any alternative; the call lasted a few minutes and addressed only the human resource implications. No one asked me what I wanted. No one other than HR talked to me at all. I never heard from my direct manager, or the managing director of the New York office—the one who'd told me how promising my trajectory was.

And that was the last day I worked on Wall Street.

There's a happy ending to this story, though it's more of a happy middle: I delivered a perfectly healthy, full-term, six-pound baby named Logan. I also took a big mental step back to think about what I really wanted professionally. My career at the investment firm was dead. Since they had nudged me out in the middle of my pregnancy—before I could put a plan in place to cover the business I had been developing—I had virtually no hope of reengaging those prospects. So I worked on my résumé between breast-feeding sessions and started interviewing when Logan was just a few weeks old. By the time he was two months, I had accepted one of three job offers, at a nonprofit that trains outstanding educators to become school leaders.

When I called my firm to resign, I worked to keep my voice level despite feeling like I'd throw up. I explained that I believed I had been the subject of pregnancy discrimination—and that I couldn't imagine returning to a workplace that treated women as I had been treated. I had one request, and that was for an exit interview with a senior manager—so I could make sure someone in a decision-making role was aware of my experience.

In hindsight, there's a fair amount of ambiguity about what *exactly* I experienced. Were the actions of my firm (or inactions, in this case) discriminatory, or were they more of an indicator of general incompetence or bureaucratic bungling? Why were so few women doing the theoretically family-friendly job I'd signed on for? Was what I'd experienced endemic? Were the men I'd worked with really that oblivious to what it takes to retain female employees? Or did they not really care about diversity, and see me (consciously or not) as a liability rather than as an asset?

Whatever it was that actually happened, I was certainly clear on how I felt: furious. I was appalled that this could happen to me—that it *had* happened to me. I weighed the long-term costs of carrying this rage around with me. I wanted to just let it go, but it wasn't going to dissipate on its own. So I pursued mediation, at the invitation of my employers.

They set up a session with a mediator and the U.S. head of my division. I arrived in the morning with my lawyer; at around three o'clock, seeing that we were on opposite sides of a very broad chasm, I walked out. Here's what I didn't have: The sense of resolution I'd hoped for. A meaningful apology. An understanding of what would change. The belief that my experience actually *meant* something.

What I *did* have: the knowledge that I'd done the right thing, and the right to tell my story.

My experience was not universal; there's no such thing as a universal experience when it comes to pregnancy and parenthood. But, despite my anxiety and heartache at being nudged out of my job, I count myself lucky. I landed on my feet: my base salary at my new job was actually *higher* than at the firm—and it was fine that I left every day at five o'clock. A year after that, I started weeSpring, finally answering the entrepreneurial calling I've felt since I was a kid.

My path hasn't been a straight-line trajectory, and none of it has been easy. (I don't think any parent would use "easy" to describe her life!) But it's been—and continues to be—both fun and fulfilling. So while I wouldn't change anything about where I've landed professionally, there are countless things I would have done differently along the way. There were a handful of things I did *right*, like realizing I'd landed myself in the wrong job and needed a path out, and not signing any post-resignation documents without consulting a lawyer. But so many things that could have been easy seemed painfully complex, like understanding short-term disability. And even the things that *seemed* simple felt fraught. Not knowing exactly which and how many forms I needed to complete gave me that pervasive sinking feeling that I'd forgotten something important. Even just telling colleagues and clients that I was pregnant was a sweat-inducing experience: When should I tell them? What should I tell them? What would they say? Then—once I returned to work—there were the logistical hurdles, like arranging a pumping schedule around meetings. I made countless missteps along the way, both big and small, and I've seen my friends and peers struggle similarly.

Federal policy is way behind the curve when it comes to protecting women. We have no national policy affording paid parental leave, which puts women and their families in significant financial binds. There are some protections against discrimination, but it's hard to prove discrimination—never mind shoulder the emotional and financial costs of litigation.

And even with groundswell political change, attitudes and culture are ingrained. As one woman put it: "People have their views on pregnant women and mothers." Often, those views have nothing to do with you, or how hard you work—and they're not going to shift overnight. So while we have to work within the reality we've got right now, know that this road has been trod before. I want this book to deliver to you that same epiphany I had when I realized several of my successful, ambitious friends were also pregnant. *You are not alone.*

In lieu of that Pregnancy and Your Professional Life class we never got, with this book I offer you a step-by-step guide to making it to the other side of motherhood with your career intact and on track. My goal is to help you avoid the landmines by sharing the stories of countless women like you who successfully traversed the minefield. And while there's no single right answer to most of the questions working mothers face, I hope the insights in this book will help you move from open-ended questions to multiple-choice ones. Consider this a Choose Your Own Adventure guide.

Back when I was in business school, I met with a woman who'd made managing director soon after her babies were born. "Live close to where you work," she told me. "Time you're spending commuting is time you're doing *neither* of the things you care about." The simplicity of that statement stuck with me, and I realized there are so many, many little things you can do to smooth your path—especially if you know what they are ahead of time.

I wanted to find out what those things were; I wanted to make it easy for other women to figure out how to make work *work*. Over the course of six months, I conducted extensive interviews with more than fifty highly successful women. I collected feedback and data from thousands more, sifting through the 1,800 pages I'd compiled of their advice. Put simply, I did the research so you don't have to.

You'll see I cite a lot of women working in big jobs at big companies, but I collected stories and insights from women all over the professional map. I heard from pastry chefs, ER doctors, legal assistants, schoolteachers, hotel managers, and nearly every other professional imaginable. Nearly 80 percent of the women who responded to my survey had income below $100,000, with about half of the total falling in the $50,000 to $99,000 range. The common thread among all is that they're invested in their professional lives. Their jobs are more than a paycheck, and they want to continue to grow in their careers.

A lot of the advice you'll find in this book is specific to the stages of pregnancy and parenthood, like sharing the news and prepping for your return. But it's also all about context; being aware—early on—of the realities of life as a working mother gives you time to make a plan. These pages are rife with quotes from women sharing what they did, or *wish* they'd done, before getting pregnant.

Part 1, Making Your Plan, covers everything you'll need to know or do before your baby arrives—whatever your situation. For any woman striving to maintain her nameplate on her desk while she brings a new baby into the world, chapters 1 and 2 detail managing pregnancy in a professional setting and preparing for maternity leave. There you'll find out how to initiate conversations with your manager and colleagues about pregnancy, and how to make sure your job gets done—well!—in your absence. The following two chapters apply to specific cases. Chapter 3 concerns women seeking a new role during pregnancy or maternity leave; chapter 4 outlines what to do should you find yourself the subject of discrimination. If you get sidelined as I was, you'll know to whom you can turn and what your options are.

Part 2, After Baby Arrives, covers your post-baby life, from making the most of maternity leave to reassimilating into the office without getting mommy-tracked. I go in-depth on childcare, because I—and many of the women I spoke with—believe that finding the right caregiver for your baby is critically important to your professional success.

Part 3, Paying It Forward, is a hands-on guide to making a difference, both for yourself and for the women who'll come after you. There you'll learn not just what you can do on an individual level, but what you can ask your company to do as well.

You can also join in the conversation at herestheplanbook.com, which has additional resources, including everything from a printable checklist of questions to ask HR to a primer on running a background check on a nanny.

So, again, while *Here's the Plan* is a play-by-play guide, it's also about preparedness. Start weaving your safety net as early as you can. Work your tail off and get ahead. As one commanding officer in the U.S. Navy said, "Pay it forward when you're young and have the energy," since that's when you're building the political and reputational capital you may need to cash in on later. But for now, in her words, "blow through their expectations." Even if you're moving on to another employer, your reputation will follow you.

Meanwhile, you can also start practicing at making your career and your personal life fit together. Even the most progressive, family-friendly company isn't going to solve that problem for you: you need to take ownership of that yourself. One woman likened the lead-up to having (and raising) children to running a marathon. "It's not about waking up and running 26.2 miles. It's getting up on Wednesday and running 3 miles, then doing 5 on Saturday." Think of this book as your trail map, letting you know where the hills are—even if you're not yet ready to run the whole course.

So let's get going!

PART 1.
MAKING
YOUR PLAN

CHAPTER 1

THE INS AND OUTS
OF FAMILY LEAVE

I n my early twenties, when all I cared about was work, pregnancy and parenthood seemed a million years away. I assumed that, when the time came, I'd be one of those women who goes into labor at the office, envisioning this as the ultimate demonstration of commitment to one's career.

Sure, when I had actual *children*, I would need to shift my priorities a bit, maybe working remotely on occasion or coming in after school drop-off a couple of days a week. But pregnancy? Pregnancy was *nothing*. I was a force of nature, and being pregnant would not slow me down.

Well, it turned out that pregnancy is a very real and literal force of nature. I saw early signs of that among my colleagues; I worked with one woman who was vomiting so much and so forcefully that she had to be put on an IV. She'd plod into the office after barfing at home for two hours, steely-eyed and determined to make it through the day, but I'd look over at her during meetings and see in her clammy, gray face that she was struggling. This was before "hyperemesis gravidarum" was a known term (made famous by the Duchess of Cambridge), so my colleague's state seemed both horrifying and rare. On the other end of the spectrum, I had heard women share—with wonder, their hands resting gently on their bellies—how pregnancy was so incredible. But even if you'll be in the happy, glowing camp, you're still looking at a prolonged absence from your job.

For that, planning is crucial, and from much earlier on than you'd expect. I have always been a planner, so naturally I had a plan for my maternity leave from my Wall Street job: I'd proactively send an email to my external contacts; I'd have a colleague keep an eye on any open accounts; I'd neatly wrap up any other loose ends; and I'd be back in the office six weeks after giving birth.

Of course, as I shared earlier, none of those things happened: I had serious complications at just 23 weeks, and I didn't set foot in my office again. In hindsight, there's not much I could have done differently; I had a plan, but I had no time to execute it.

What *would* have made a difference would have been understanding and accepting that there's nothing reliably predictable about pregnancy. We're regularly told what "usually" happens when one is pregnant: if you suffer from morning sickness, you'll usually start to feel better around 12 weeks; women usually love the second trimester; first pregnancies usually deliver a little late. But here's the thing: you might be unusual—in fact, in some regard you probably will be. So advance planning is essential.

The first step is wrapping your head around what your time away from work will mean for you.

WHAT TIME AWAY MEANS

I talked to dozens of women who felt deep, bone-shaking anxiety about taking maternity leave. Some were panicked at the thought of a three-month black hole of work left untouched during their absence. Others were concerned about their career trajectory, especially if making accommodations for that leave would require them to start saying "no." For some, the "no" wasn't just about broadly declining additional responsibility; it was tied to very specific and practical things that would be impossible. For example: "No, I can't be in Dallas in March because I'm having a baby in February," or, "No, I won't be able to lead the due diligence on that deal because I'll be on maternity leave for half of it."

And given the sorry state of paid leave in our country—which I'll outline in detail—there are also major financial implications to taking leave. One woman wanted to take the full time she was afforded under the Family and Medical Leave Act (twelve weeks), but was eligible for only six weeks of *paid* leave—so she took the other six weeks unpaid. "Your financial life stops," she said, "for almost fifty days."

> "After trying for seven years to have a baby, it never occurred to me to think about what would happen when I did."
> —A NONPROFIT CEO, NEW YORK CITY

For other women, the fear took a more ominous tone: they feared they'd fooled everyone into believing they were valuable. If they left, what would happen if no one missed them? Would it finally become clear to their colleagues that they weren't really contributing? This is a classic example of impostor syndrome, wherein one feels incompetent or unqualified—and on the verge of being exposed as such. In *The Secret Thoughts of Successful Women: Why Capable People Suffer from the Impostor Syndrome and How to Thrive in Spite of It*, Dr. Valerie Young profiles countless household names who have feared they're frauds, including Maya Angelou, Tina Fey, and Meryl Streep. Sheryl Sandberg also discusses it in *Lean In*. Impostor syndrome is painfully common in women.

And then there are the women who truly believed (and in many cases rightfully so) that their companies couldn't operate without them. Not working meant that whatever they'd been doing would come to a screeching halt. The most talked-about instance of this was Marissa Mayer's highly publicized two-week maternity leave, which was scheduled to happen just a few months after she'd been named

CEO of Yahoo. I remember that news cycle as a whirlwind of contradictions, with comments like "It's groundbreaking that a pregnant woman has been named CEO of a public company!" being countered by "It's destructive of her to be suggesting women don't need to recover after childbirth!"

During my first pregnancy, I felt I'd be leaving my company (and career) in the lurch, and so I declared I'd take minimal leave. At the time I was a sole operator in a commission-based business-development role, which meant if I didn't do something, it didn't get done. I landed on that six weeks estimate by interrogating a woman who'd just had her third baby. She told me, very bluntly, that it wasn't an option for her to take time off. "I'd lose my clients. They expect to hear from *me*, not an assistant." She hired a baby nurse and worked from home.

The second time around, I was running a startup—and I took a different approach. Soon after I shared that I was pregnant, I started moving things off my plate and onto others'. First I created an extensive document of my responsibilities (which is a good exercise for anyone, pregnant or not). I prioritized the responsibilities, and identified a new "owner" for many of them. I then shared this document on the cloud with the team, so everyone could see who was handling what. This process also shored up their confidence that we could hold things together without my being involved in the day-to-day operations.

But the most empowering, and unexpected, benefit of this planning was that a lot of things didn't get a new owner. They just didn't get done. The exercise was enlightening, forcing me to identify what I spent time on that wasn't mission-critical. Sending a monthly email update to investors? A good idea, certainly, but they'd be fine with quarterly updates. Leading content syndication deals with partner sites? While that could be a game changer if I pulled it off, it was also a huge long shot—and I couldn't afford to invest my time in long shots. Other women echoed how illuminating it was to just stop doing part of their job and discover there were limited consequences. One referred to the startling revelation that parts of her job "could get iced for three months if they had to be."

Of course, this kind of streamlining becomes second nature once you're juggling your work life and your kids, but it's a powerful thing to act on while pregnant because it gives you a preview of your office during your absence. One woman started working from home two days a week *during* her pregnancy, essentially running a maternity drill for her team. "I wanted them to get some practice at not having me around while I could still keep an eye on things." Similarly, taking stock of the nonessentials—and putting them on the back burner—before you take leave gives you a chance to assess whether or not the company can operate without them.

Another thing to consider: whether you'll want or need to take some time off prior to the birth of your child. Those federally mandated twelve weeks can start to shrink if you want or need to tap into those days before delivering. Some women are emphatic that you should work up until you deliver—not just to show commitment to your career, but also because it buys you more time with the baby. Their decisions were compounded by the fact that they weren't sure when they'd deliver, so they could wind up miscalculating by two weeks or more. They said things like, "I didn't want to waste my maternity leave." But others felt that pre-baby time couldn't be further from "waste"—that it's absolutely essential to give yourself the physical and mental break before embarking on what one woman referred to as "the road to perpetual exhaustion." And some women had no choice at all: for medical reasons, they had to bow out of work early. One woman I interviewed delivered at 28 weeks, then returned to work six weeks later while her baby was still in the neonatal intensive-care unit. Though that period was harrowing and miserable, with that early return she was able to take her remaining six weeks once her baby came home from the hospital.

Some short-term disability policies will cover things like pregnancy bed rest without diminishing your maternity leave, but that's a question only your HR department can answer. You'll also want to ask HR what your leave options are. That's covered lower down, starting with "Overview of Family Leave in the U.S." Some fortunate women have a say in how they'll structure their leave. Lately companies have started making headlines by announcing extended leave policies, such as offering flexibility for paid time to be used at any point up until baby's first birthday, or, in the case of Netflix, offering "unlimited" time off.

For women who are afforded choice, the next step is figuring out how long you can afford—professionally, financially, and emotionally—to take time away from career life.

HOW LONG IS ENOUGH? HOW LONG IS TOO MUCH?

To get right to the point: deciding on the length of your maternity leave *before* you've had a baby is completely backwards. For one thing, you're about to undergo the biggest life change you'll ever face, commencing with a physical feat I've heard some women equate with running a marathon without any training. Regardless of how prepared you think you are, there's really no way to predict how you're going to feel mentally and physically—never mind deciding when you'll be ready to return to business as usual. So if you get to choose the length of your leave, you have to make that choice blindly.

Because there's no broadly mandated paid leave in the U.S., duration of maternity leave is primarily a financial decision for many families. To give yourself more flexibility on the financial side, one woman advised starting a separate bank account pre-baby and diverting a portion of your take-home pay into it so you have a fund you can dip into in those weeks or months with no paycheck. If you're not yet pregnant, I cannot emphasize this enough: start *now*.

PAID MATERNITY LEAVE IS NOT A GIVEN

Countless women told me that they were floored to learn that their companies didn't offer fully paid maternity leave. Many received no pay at all, while others received just 60 percent of their paychecks for six weeks. One academic told me, "I financed my maternity leave with a credit card."

Every year, *Working Mother* magazine publishes a survey of the top 100 employers for women; in addition to stats on teleworking and the number of women executives, it includes data on the amount of parental leave offered. Of the 100 companies considered most friendly to working women, only 18 percent offered twelve or more weeks fully paid. More (19 percent) had only four weeks of leave paid in full, with the average landing at just 7.5 weeks. And that's the most hospitable companies!

Brittany Griffin is a former teacher who now works at an education-focused technology company. She was pleasantly shocked to learn they covered twelve weeks at full salary, but she saw it as an embarrassment of riches. She had friends who worked in medicine who had to go back before their C-sections had fully healed; another friend who was a waitress started taking shifts a week after her baby was born. "I couldn't tell any of my friends I had twelve weeks paid," she said. "I don't know anyone who got their full salary for that long."

Jane Barratt, founder of GoldBean and the former head of a global advertising agency, told me that she financed a yearlong maternity leave by selling half of the Apple stock she'd bought in her twenties.

Twelve weeks is usually what you'll see in companies where the leave policy is considered generous. Anecdotally, I found that companies that needed to be aggressive in recruiting top talent (like big law firms, who all compete against each other for top law school graduates) offered the "cushiest" packages. But the policy on the books and what people actually do can be vastly different. One lawyer shared, "It's nice if you can actually afford to step away from your duties for that long," but most women can't.

"Three months is nothing," one senior executive told me. "Nothing!" But because most people in major corporations don't take more than one week of vacation at a time, it feels like an eternity—both to them and to their colleagues. The reality is that "few projects get done in three months, especially at big companies." It's less time than you think, both for the work you're missing and the time you're taking at home.

But while the difference between three months and four months may seem minimal, it's incrementally huge for your newborn. At four months, she's a "little less fragile," as one of the moms I talked to phrased it, and she has more set rhythms. Your body is healed, and you're probably feeling a little more confident. You're probably also getting significantly more sleep—all of which benefits your baby.

Unfortunately, some companies have zero flexibility on this timeline. When one global marketing manager requested an unpaid extension on her leave, they flatly refused. "I hadn't slept for twelve weeks, and I couldn't give them a clear answer about how much more time I would need." She thought it might have been two weeks, or maybe two months—but she realizes now that by being nonspecific she put herself in a poor negotiating position. The company told her they couldn't hold her job, but she could resign and then call as soon as she was ready to come back. So that's what she did, thinking it would be a quick reentry—but because the financial crisis hit around that same time, it wound up taking years.

While I'm not trying to fearmonger here, it's worth doing your research now to determine what the contingencies would be should you want or need more time off. Ask other women who took leave, or talk to HR in broad terms about whether there's flexibility if the family needs it. These conversations, particularly with people who have influence over your job, can be a tricky balance: you don't want to signal any doubts about returning, but you also need context on policy and precedent if you're going to try to secure an extension.

You can also survey other women in your industry to get a sense of what's considered normal. The CMO of a publicly traded multinational company asked every senior-level mother in her organization—and friends outside—how they maximized their time, extended their leave beyond what was allocated on the books, and prepared for their departure. "There's just no playbook for an executive leaving for three months." Her research turned up a blood-boiling disparity: in France, employees of her company could take nine months' paid leave, and there was a woman at her same level currently taking that length of leave at her full salary. But because she was in New York she was entitled to only three months, and even if she *could* take more, she feared it wouldn't go over culturally. She ultimately took five months, using vacation days, personal days, and banking every other day possible for her maternity leave. The risk there, though, is that you go back with no accrued leave, so if your child is sick—or you are—you have to take an unpaid day.

Another woman, a partner in a venture capital firm where there were no other women, didn't have a precedent to go by. She was pretty sure she wanted to take significant time with her new baby, but her partners were all married to women who stayed home full-time. She knew they already anticipated her departure—and not constructively so. In her first year one of her partners tried to dissuade her from attending an expensive conference. When she pressed him he said, "You could be here for eighteen months, go have a baby, and never come back. It's not good ROI to spend $5,000 for you to go to this conference." She was stunned, but took this as an early view at the partners' mentality.

So she conducted a thorough analysis before she told them she was pregnant. "I knew that I would have to go above and beyond on planning and logistics," she said, "and it had to be in a way that would make sense to them." Fortunately she had a mentor, who worked at a different firm, who surreptitiously passed along data on the maternity leaves of a dozen women from other small investment funds, including how long they took and whether they were paid. Armed with that, she presented to her partners a one-page document with a bullet point reading, "[initials] at full salary for Q4" ("Q4" being her euphemism for "twelve-week maternity leave"). She spoke in their language, and it worked; they didn't even blink at that line.

For some, policy *is* malleable. When media executive Fran Hauser sat down with her company's HR specialist to discuss her maternity leave, she was shocked to learn she was eligible for only three or four weeks of the official maternity policy of thirteen weeks. Why? She was adopting, and the company didn't consider it comparable. "I'm bringing home a newborn!" she told them. "I don't understand why there's a difference." She fought it, enlisting her boss and another senior woman who'd adopted a child a decade earlier, and she won: the policy was changed company-wide. She felt she owed it to the other women she worked with, knowing that someone more junior raising this issue might not have succeeded. "I had a lot of women reporting in to me," she said. "I was a mentor to them. It was my responsibility to speak up."

A Preview of Post-Baby Capacity

In thinking about how much time you'll need, the other major consideration is what life with a newborn actually looks like. I was clueless on this: I'd heard from friends that it was hard (obviously), but I was cloudy on *what* would be hard. The concrete things, like "You won't have time to take a shower," sounded like hyperbole. I knew people who'd had rough physical recoveries, and I'd heard complaints about lack of sleep, but I didn't really have a sense of how that would affect me.

What wound up surprising me most was the enormous, radical impact of sleep deprivation. While we're told newborns need to eat every two hours, we're not always told those two hours are start-time to start-time. A breast-feeding newborn can take forty-five minutes to nurse. If you add in a diaper change, a trip to the bathroom, and a snack for you, you're down to about an hour. So for those first couple of weeks, on average you're getting sleep in one-hour increments.

That sleep deprivation has myriad effects. It'll affect your appetite (you're more likely to crave sugary foods) and your mood, but its most tremendous impact is on your cognition. The underslept brain doesn't store new memories (like what your boss said in that meeting) as effectively, and suffers from diminished word recall. Sleep deprivation reduces your ability to concentrate, which will compound those memory problems further. It also impacts your decision-making: studies have shown that after a night of interrupted sleep, people are less risk-averse and more likely to make rash decisions—a phenomenon all-night casinos bank on. (We'll cover the how and why of sleep deprivation in more detail later.)

Needless to say, this isn't a mental state that'll be constructive for your professional work, but too few companies consider this when setting their parental-leave policies.

Soon after my son was born, I vividly remember thinking—in abject desperation—that it would be twenty years before I again got more than two contiguous hours of sleep. Thankfully I was wrong, and by the time I went back to work at twelve weeks, Logan was usually waking up only once between 8:00 PM and 6:00 AM. But even that left me less than sharp.

There's no such thing as "normal" when it comes to infant sleep, but we know a few things that researchers believe apply almost universally. First, circadian rhythms aren't established until newborns are at least four months old—so until then, your baby can't really differentiate between night and day. Second, the length of time babies can go between feedings (which also is the maximum they'll sleep in one stretch) is tied to weight, not age, which makes it even harder to predict when you'll achieve some regularity. So no matter how successful you've been in other parts of your life, infant sleep is not something you'll be able to shoehorn into a rigid schedule.

Take that into account when you're thinking about both your return-to-work date and your return-to-work plan. If you can factor in some flexibility—like a later start-time so you can grab a catnap in the morning, or some work-from-home days—it could *improve* your performance by helping you get the rest you need to function effectively.

Childcare Logistics

The ins and outs of managing childcare as a working parent are laid out in Chapter 6: Hiring a Caregiver, but how you'll handle that transition should also factor into your thinking about your leave from work. Katie Duffy, CEO of Democracy Prep Public Schools, told me she couldn't imagine staying away from work for twelve weeks. "Both our HR manager and my mom hassled me to think more wisely, so I messaged my leave as twelve weeks because I thought I would be back well before then." But her childcare search pushed that out another two weeks, to fourteen total, because she hadn't allowed time for that search early on. "I was working from home early on in my maternity leave," she said, "when I should have been screening nannies." Another woman told me she wished she'd built in more overlap time—so she'd still be at home when her nanny started taking care of her daughter—to give her time to get comfortable and build rapport with her caregiver. For parents taking their child to daycare, you might also want to consider reserving some of your leave for days your baby won't be able to go in; you'll soon learn how common both daycare facility holidays and unplanned sickness can be.

However you chart your childcare, there's still a huge emotional hurdle to overcome: leaving your child with someone else. There's just no way to know how you'll feel about it until you're in it, so consider preserving what flexibility you can.

Leave for "Secondary Caregivers" (a.k.a. Paternity Leave)

I bristle at the term "secondary caregivers" because it implies that someone is a "primary" caregiver and that parenting responsibilities aren't divided equally. Cynthia Calvert, president of Workforce 21C and a senior advisor to the Center for WorkLife Law, advises companies to avoid terms like "secondary" and "nonprimary" caregiver in their leave policies because of the challenges inherent in enforcing a categorization like that. "Do they really want to police who is a primary and who is a secondary?"

But putting aside what it's called when someone who wasn't the birth mother takes time to bond with a baby, studies have shown that women whose spouses take parental leave have a lower incidence of postpartum depression and are also more likely to earn more over the course of their career.[1] If his or her company is covered by the Family and Medical Leave Act (discussed below), your spouse or coparent is eligible for the same twelve weeks of unpaid leave that you are; some more progressive companies, like Facebook and Change.org, offer several months of paid parental leave for *all* parents. (That said, 65 percent of the women I heard from reported that their spouses had no paid parental leave—not even a measly week.)

But leave "offered" and leave "accepted" are still a long way apart: one of my friends told me that when her husband applied for parental leave he was ribbed by his colleagues. She was astonished. "It's a family-friendly company," she said. "All of these guys have kids." It turned out that, while they *were* taking some time off when their children were born (one or two weeks, usually), no one was classifying it as parental leave. My friend told me—with considerable pride—about how her husband jumped through a series of bureaucratic hoops to get approved for his "parental bonding time," as the company called it. "He was sending a signal that it's important to afford that time to *both* parents." Fathers filing for parental leave also demonstrate to their companies that having a baby isn't solely a mother's responsibility.

A new-father friend of mine took six weeks, saying: "It didn't even feel like a decision. I was just going to do it." He acknowledged, though, that it's a luxury to think about paternity leave as a foregone conclusion. "I was just at the right company, at the right time, with the right people who shared my values."

Many companies that offer paid parental leave will allow the parent to take that leave anytime in the first year after a child is born. A number of women I interviewed passed the parenting baton to their significant other after their own leave ended, at which time their spouses took a few weeks (and in some cases, a few months) to care for their three-month-old. "Partners can tag in and out," one nonprofit executive said.

Never Enough Time

In soliciting insights and advice for this book—from hard-charging women, doing impressive jobs in a wide array of fields—I assumed most would be itching to get back to the office, eager to return to familiar routines and the satisfaction that comes from executing your job well.

Of course, there were plenty of those women, and I counted myself among them after my first pregnancy. I had gotten lonely, particularly because my husband started his MBA—which is a twelve-plus-hour daily commitment in the beginning—just days after Logan was born. After months alone with a newborn, I was hungry for some professional validation. My best friend from business school told a similar story: "I realized during maternity leave how much I thrive on feeling competent and smart and capable. Suddenly, I found myself in a situation where I didn't know what I was doing. And all I wanted was to go do something I knew I was good at!"

But the *vast* majority said the time they took wasn't enough— nowhere near enough—and would have taken more time if it had been financially or professionally viable to do so. "A twelve-week-old baby is just so, so tiny," one woman lamented. "I couldn't wrap my head around handing her over to a virtual stranger, but I had to do it." Others had challenging recoveries, and felt they spent most of their leave trying to heal physically—with no real time left to "enjoy" their babies once they felt well enough to do so.

That healing is emotional, too. Three months after my second pregnancy I was gearing up to return to my startup when postpartum depression hit. Though I was mostly fine—in contrast to many—I was incredibly emotional. I was so grateful I had the luxury of working from home, which meant I could work around those tearful periods *and* get in a daytime nap.

So, again, for those women fortunate enough to have some leeway in the leave they can take, there are a number of different factors to consider. Coming up, I discuss the more nitty-gritty aspects of family leave, including both how to assess what your specific options will be and how to negotiate the best deal you can get. But first, let's consider the FMLA.

OVERVIEW OF FAMILY LEAVE IN THE U.S.

Here's some basic background on pregnancy and work in the United States.

The 1993 Family and Medical Leave Act (FMLA) guarantees up to twelve weeks of unpaid leave to recover from a serious health condition or to care for a newborn or adopted child or sick family member. It applies only to those who've worked with an organization or company for twelve months or more, and many small businesses (defined as having fewer than fifty employees) are exempt. In all, about 60 percent of the workforce is covered by the FMLA. Note that no provisions in the FMLA require that your employer pay you while you are on leave.

Rules at the state level can vary—and some are more generous to pregnant employees. Some states enforce the core provisions of the FMLA for companies with more than ten or fifteen employees, and a few states, like California, New Jersey, and Rhode Island, mandate some paid leave.

If you do have paid leave, it can come in all shapes and sizes. Some get their full salaries, some get a percentage; some get a few weeks, some get a few months. Your employer may pay you directly, or they might offer short-term disability insurance, which pays your salary or a portion thereof during leave. And though short-term disability varies by insurance provider and policy, generally it applies to both pregnancy complications and postpartum recovery. The amount of time a disability insurer will give you is capped; for a vaginal birth it's usually six weeks; for a C-section it's eight weeks. About 60 percent of the women I surveyed for this book received some short-term disability.

That's something few people understand: if you anticipate getting pregnant in the next few years and have the opportunity to enroll in short-term disability insurance through your employer, *get the most generous policy available.* For a long time I conflated disability and long-term care, which I thought was just relevant for elderly people, but my short-term disability paid my salary for four months while I was on pregnancy bed rest.

In the states where everyone has access to paid family leave, that leave is funded by payroll deductions that pool into a statewide insurance policy. Like unemployment, the amount you're paid during leave is capped at both a percentage of your salary and an absolute weekly benefit. In New Jersey, for instance, you could receive a maximum $604 in 2014.

Some employers step in and supplement your insurance- or state-provided disability. They might make you "whole" if your insurance only covers 60 percent of your salary, or they may opt to pay you directly for X weeks or months after your paid disability leave runs out.

All of that said, according to a report issued in 2014 by the Council of Economic Advisers, 28 percent of college-educated women receive zero paid leave.[2] And these women surprisingly often have high-level jobs that you'd expect would afford paid leave as a benefit. A nuclear engineer who served in the U.S. Navy told me: "I haven't yet found a company that has paid maternity leave. If there was one with six weeks of paid leave, I'd probably be working there!" When she had a baby, she couldn't afford to sacrifice her salary for more than a month, so she started teleworking when her newborn was just four weeks old.

I want to let that sink in for a minute. A highly trained, highly specialized former Navy officer couldn't find a job that offered any paid family leave, and so to pay her mortgage she had to return to work just one month after childbirth.

UNDERSTANDING YOUR EMPLOYEE HANDBOOK

Your employee handbook is the best place to start educating yourself on what's ahead. (Note that *handbook* has become a misnomer, as it's usually found on a company- or organization-wide intranet.) Unfortunately, at too many companies the official policy is opaque: they may tell you how much leave you can take, but not how much you'll be paid during that time. One woman said, "The company policy is about a paragraph long. It didn't tell me any of the specifics." (Later, in the section "Crafting Your Leave and Negotiating It," you'll find a sidebar advising you what to do if your company doesn't have a maternity leave policy.)

I've seen policies that say you're eligible for twelve weeks of leave under the employer's short-term disability benefit, but that fail to specify that the disability benefit for childbirth will cover only a maximum of eight weeks' recovery time (and that's for a C-section). If you didn't know to ask, you'd likely assume you'd get paid for all twelve weeks.

I've noticed too that the language can be brusque and alienating, even when it's in line with the tone used elsewhere. One government handbook reads: "There is no separate leave category called maternity leave. Leave for maternity reasons is a combination of as many as three separate kinds of leave: sick leave, annual leave, and leave without pay (LWOP)." A major media company requires that "the employee can certify that she is the 'primary caregiver' of the child and, as such, is responsible for the feeding, clothing, bathing, changing, and health of the child," but doesn't explain what this certification would entail. (Do they think employees are contracting themselves out as surrogates so they can bilk the company's maternity leave policy?)

One woman I talked to learned she was pregnant three weeks after starting a new job at Yahoo. Though their generous new maternity policy was much touted (after the backlash they weathered when they eliminated their work-from-home policy), she couldn't find information on when she'd be eligible for that leave. Was it immediate, and for all employees? Or did she have to be in her job for twelve months before she could take advantage of it? The short answer for her: everyone was eligible, regardless of tenure at the company. But that's not always the case. One prominent New York financial services company gives twelve weeks of paid leave, unless you've been there less than one year, in which case you get just eight weeks. "I've taken two maternity leaves at my company," one health care employee told me, "and I'm still not sure how they pay you. It almost feels like they don't even want you to know what's available to you."

In some cases, the language is convoluted and complicated because companies are trying to comply with Title VII of the 1964 Civil Rights Act, which protects against sex discrimination. They're required to give the same amount of paid "baby-bonding time" to women and men, though they are allowed to offer separate "childbirth-recovery time" exclusively to birth mothers. (Typically, six to eight weeks is considered the recovery time for an uncomplicated birth.) So they have layers upon layers of designations of the types of leave women may take—and how those women will be compensated during those particular layers of leave.

There's so much confusion and ambiguity in company policies on parental leave that one enterprising expectant mother at a big financial services company—which has a reputation for being especially friendly to new mothers—created a PowerPoint document to clarify the policy and process. It included everything you need to know or do for maternity leave there, and it was passed around informally, friend to friend. If a company that's considered progressive on family matters needs to have its policy voluntarily repackaged by an employee so it can be actually understood, we probably across the board need to revisit the way employers communicate with workers about their health and family life.

ASSESSING YOUR LEAVE OPTIONS

When the time comes to discuss your pregnancy with your employer, deciding whom you tell first—Human Resources or your manager— really depends on your relationship with your manager. Most of the women I talked to felt it was important to have their direct manager be the first to know at the company, but some wanted a clear understanding of what the company policy was before talking to their supervisor. Some women get the lay of the land by talking to a discreet coworker who recently had a baby. (If you opt to talk first with HR or a new-parent colleague, you may want to state up-front that you'd like to be the one to share the news with your manager.) I cover sharing your pregnancy with your boss and colleagues later on; for now, let's look at the fine print of what your leave options are.

Regardless of when you speak to HR, don't treat the initial meeting with them as the phase when you volley for what you need—that comes later. (And how to do so is covered in the section "Crafting Your Leave and Negotiating It.") Treat the initial meeting with them as a fact-finding mission. Take notes throughout the conversation, and send an email afterward confirming your understanding of the policy. This is especially important: since few companies have a comprehensive policy in writing, there could be significant ambiguity, for instance, around your compensation model. If your compensation is partly based on commission off previous business, how will you receive those payments while on leave? If you are eligible for an annual bonus, is your bonus pool reduced because you're working only 75 percent of the year?

When you're ready, start by broadly inquiring about the company's parental leave policy, and then get specific.

QUESTIONS TO ASK HR

How You Get Paid

- What is the maximum amount of time away, including extended unpaid time, that the company allows?
- Do I have flexibility in how I use that time? Can I apply some of that time to working part-time once I return or reserve some of my leave for later?
- How much of my salary will I receive while on leave?
- Does my equity continue to vest while I'm on parental leave? [*This is especially important if your equity represents a large portion of your compensation.*]
- [*If you are in a state that affords parental leave*] Does my state-sponsored leave occur concurrently with my employer-sponsored leave, or is it sequential?
- If you offer incentive-based compensation, how does that work?
- Am I still eligible for my full bonus, or is it a pro-rata share?
- How will commissions be paid out while I am on leave?

How Benefits Are Handled

- How is my health insurance paid for while I'm on leave? [*If your leave is unpaid, you may have to mail in a check for your portion of your health insurance.*] What about contributions to Flexible Spending Accounts?
- [*If you have life insurance or disability insurance through your company*] How is my life insurance paid?
- Do I accrue benefits while out on leave? [*Ask about retirement fund contributions, vacation days or sick days, time toward a sabbatical, and any other benefits your employer may offer.*]

- What are the terms of my short-term disability coverage?
- What happens if I have medical complications and need to leave early? How much of my salary will I receive?
- If I did have to leave early, would that count as part of my maternity leave?

The Nitty-Gritty Logistics

- What forms do I need to complete, and when?
- When is the FMLA form due?
- Is there a form for short-term disability?
- When do I need to finalize my departure and return dates?
- How do I make changes to my health insurance, like adding my child and adjusting my Flexible Spending Account (FSA) elections? What is the deadline for doing this?
- Do you offer a Dependent Care Flexible Spending Account? How does that work?
- How do I add my child as a beneficiary on my retirement account and employer-provided life insurance?

Your Return to Work

- Does the company allow teleworking or flex-time?
- Are there mothers' rooms or other facilities for pumping moms? [*Ask to see them. You can find a checklist of things to look for on page 194.*]
- Are there any other benefits for new parents that I should be aware of?

(You can find a printable PDF of these questions on herestheplanbook.com.)

You can—and should—ask these types of questions of HR after you've been extended a job offer (though most women I spoke with cautioned to wait until you have an offer letter in hand).

One very, very important note: remember that HR's job is to protect the company, not you. "Use them to your advantage," one woman advised, "but don't ever think they're on your side." HR is supposed to be the voice of reason to smooth everything over, and that kind of placating can lull you into thinking that they're your ally or advocate. "They're no one person's advocate," she continued. "They don't care about personal issues, no matter how friendly they sound." Their primary responsibility is to the corporation or organization you work for.

CRAFTING YOUR LEAVE, AND NEGOTIATING IT

"Having a child has meant that I really calculate the value of the time I'm spending away from my daughter. It's made me so much more emboldened to ask for what I'm worth, rather than what someone will give me."

—A PARTNER IN A VENTURE CAPITAL FIRM

Once you've done your homework and understand the lay of the land you'll be working with, the next step is to consider what would work best for you—and then to negotiate for that. In determining what you'll want to negotiate, I recommend listing the details of both your leave (how long you'll be gone, and how you'll be compensated) and your return to work (where, when, and how much you'll work). (See "Considerations for Your Parental Leave and Return to Work" sidebar.)

How to negotiate effectively is a far deeper topic than I can cover in this section, so if you haven't received any formal training in negotiation, consider picking up a copy of Roger Fisher and William L. Ury's *Getting to Yes: Negotiating Agreement Without Giving In*, which is widely considered essential business reading. And this isn't just for

CONSIDERATIONS FOR YOUR PARENTAL LEAVE AND RETURN TO WORK

Your Parental Leave

LENGTH OF LEAVE: Think about both paid and unpaid time. The amount of paid time off may not be negotiable, but some women cobble together extended leave using vacation or sick days. You might also ask to log some on-duty hours during your leave (like two hours, twice a week) that you can use to add a few more days to the end of your leave. Get creative, and propose some ideas. (For more, see the "For Those Who Have a Choice: How Long Is Enough? How Long Is Too Much?" section earlier in this chapter.)

HOW YOU'LL BE COMPENSATED: The size of your salary is the obvious consideration, but also think about bonus structures, commissions, and additional compensation for overtime.

Your Return to Work

WHERE YOU'LL WORK: Do you want flexibility to work from somewhere other than your main office? This can be a regularly scheduled arrangement (like working from home every Thursday), or it can be something you call upon when you need it (like when your child is sick). If you're open to considering relocation, put that on the list.

WHEN YOU'LL WORK: Will you continue to work traditional hours, or would you like the freedom to work in blocks of time that fit around your family obligations? Also consider your vacation time and allotment of personal days, though they may be rigidly assigned based on company policy.

HOW MUCH YOU'LL WORK: Do you want to scale back your hours for a period of time (or maybe even increase them)? What would

→

that look like: four days a week, or leaving at 3:00 PM daily, or something else? If you have paid parental leave, can you use that leave in a flexible way, like working part-time after you return? Are there any job-sharing arrangements you can take advantage of?

OTHER PERKS: Does your employer help offset childcare costs or provide backup childcare?

discussing leave time: this is applicable for conversations about flexibility, compensation, and more.

Most of the advice below applies to negotiating with either HR or your direct manager. (Sometimes you can work out a side deal with your manager that doesn't involve HR at all, like getting permission to work remotely one day a week.)

Lay the groundwork for your negotiation well before you sit down at the table. A successful investor told me, "From the time I was hired, I set out to make myself as indispensable as possible so I would have as much negotiating leverage as possible when I got pregnant." Another woman advised building relationships with both HR and legal; she hadn't done so consciously, but after seven years at her company she'd developed friendly rapport with leaders on both teams. "It helped," she said. "You don't want to meet someone for the first time when you're negotiating a maternity package."

The core premise to consider, especially when you're talking about your family life, is that negotiating isn't always a zero-sum game, where your loss is their win and vice versa. Experts talk about reaching the "efficient frontier," where you're maximizing the value that each party is deriving from the negotiation.

You can get there by identifying *everything* that's on the table—and on your list. Once you have a comprehensive list of what's up for negotiation, look for places where you can derive value without it "costing" your employer anything. The beauty of capitalizing on the efficient frontier is that there may be must-haves on your list that don't directly add costs to their bottom line (like five additional personal days), or your employer may have a budget line like "professional development" that could be used to compensate you indirectly. One startup VP asked for—and received—professional development funds that she could allocate toward the cost of childcare when she traveled for conferences. "A straight-up raise didn't meet my objectives," she explained, "but they wanted to retain me, so we got creative."

Progressive companies are getting more and more thoughtful about flexibility—in both hours and location. "Productivity happens in more places than just the office," explained Jennifer Hill, COO of a health care data startup. "Companies that focus on output tend to yield more appreciative and productive companies. The future is companies integrating with life instead of blocking it."

Frame everything on your list in terms of what's in it for them. For example, you could say:

- "Working remotely two days a week eliminates my commuting time, so I get an hour back in my schedule on those days to get ahead on XYZ projects."
- "Shifting my schedule so I'm working a couple of hours in the late evenings will help me focus on the XYZ initiative, because I can work uninterrupted by calls or meetings."

You'll also want to put yourself in their shoes, imagining what their objections might be. Be systematic about this too: write everything down. Come up with a comprehensive list, and then develop a response for each one. "It's just like a sales process," a professional coach told me. You identify objections in advance, and have ready a thoughtful counterpoint to each.

Jennifer Dulski, the CEO of Change.org, often delivers speeches to women and men early in their careers. When asked about how to achieve balance in working life, she gives them two pieces of advice. The first is to be great at your job. "Overdeliver when asked for things," she tells them. "Be the one with the solution when problems arise." And the second: once you're great at your job, don't ask permission. You still need to *tell* someone when you'll be away and keep lines of communication open about your projects and accessibility, but frame those conversations with care. "I never said, 'Can I leave at noon and come back at 3:00?' If you're asking permission, you're making it seem like your employer has a choice." But, and this goes back to the first point, if you're great at your job, you've earned some latitude. She reiterated, though, that you can only get away with this if you really deliver. "You have to be 200 percent confident that you will be able to do the things you've promised and more."

Do not, I repeat, *do not* make apologies at any point in your conversations with your employer about your pregnancy or early parenthood. Just state the facts, without apology. Replace "I'm sorry I won't be able to make it to that meeting" with a simple "I won't be able to make it to that meeting."

Women make apologies compulsively, and they're often not even aware that they're doing it.[3] Case in point: after a presentation I made to a group of investors, a woman pulled me aside to say, "I don't know if you realized it, but you apologized about a half dozen times in your ten-minute talk." I had offhandedly apologized for my font size, the amount of information I had on one slide, and the fact that I wasn't projecting to the back of the room—none of which merited an apology. And don't just watch out for "I'm sorry"; using crutch words like "just" (as in, "I just wanted to check in . . .") is an implicit apology. You don't need them. Be direct, be assertive, and be done with it.

And before you walk into that room, watch Amy Cuddy's TED talk about power posing. She's done research demonstrating that when you *feel* powerful, you'll be more confident—and one way to feel powerful is through your posture.

IF YOUR COMPANY DOESN'T HAVE
A MATERNITY LEAVE POLICY

If you're working in a small company or organization, there's a fair chance they don't officially have anything on the books about maternity leave. (I talked to several women tasked with setting up a maternity leave policy during their pregnancies.) If this is the case for you, you have a great opportunity—not only to set yourself up, but also to ensure that every woman who comes after you can bond with her new baby without being thrown into financial turmoil.

The two corporate policies I point to most often are those of Google and Vodafone. Google's family-friendly approach is often credited to Susan Wojcicki, a mother of five who was Google's sixteenth employee and is now CEO of YouTube. Wojcicki wrote in *The Wall Street Journal* that, when Google increased their maternity package from twelve to eighteen weeks, they saw a 50 percent increase in retention. And Vodafone made news when they announced a global policy of sixteen weeks of paid leave, followed by six months of thirty-hour weeks—all at full salary.

Again, this isn't just about asking for something for yourself. This is helping to set up your company for success by establishing a policy that will help them recruit and retain top talent, while also ensuring that the women in your company are afforded maternity leave. (There's a reason I'm beating this point home: research has shown that when women are negotiating on behalf of someone else, they do so more effectively.) And this isn't just about women, so talk about "parental leave," not maternity leave. Plus, if you're talking to a male supervisor, he may be more empathetic if he's hearing language that feels inclusive to him (even if only unconsciously).

→

Some other basic principles of negotiation apply here as well:

- FRAME EVERYTHING IN TERMS OF WHY IT'S GOOD FOR BUSINESS. Companies that offer paid family leave aren't just doing right by their employees; they're helping their bottom line by reducing costly employee turnover. [*Here you could cite Susan Wojcicki's Google stat (noted above) about increased retention.*] They're also increasing their profile when it comes to recruiting *new* talent; for instance, since big law firms actively compete with each other to hire top graduates, they almost universally have generous parental-leave packages.

- ANCHOR THE CONVERSATION BY PUTTING YOUR RECOMMENDATION ON THE TABLE FIRST, AND PROPOSE MORE THAN YOU THINK IS FAIR. If your goal is twelve weeks of paid leave, explain why sixteen weeks is optimal for both employees and employers. (Because babies are *just* starting to establish rhythms at twelve weeks, allowing parents to be at home with a new baby until sixteen weeks gives them time to find some stability in their routines and sleep patterns. A parent returning sixteen weeks post-birth will be better rested, more confident about parenting, and more capable of being apart from her baby for eight or more hours a day. This translates to a more effective, focused, and dedicated worker.)

- REMEMBER THAT A NEGOTIATION ISN'T A ZERO-SUM GAME, WHERE EVERYTHING YOU WIN IS A LOSS TO THE OTHER PARTY. Sometimes there are things on the table that one party values greatly (like flexibility to work from home one or two days a week, or ability to spread part of your paid leave over time) that come at virtually no cost to the other party.

Prior to this conversation, you'll want to research your company's short-term disability policy (if it has one), as well as your state's rules about family leave, so you'll have a clear understanding of what the out-of-pocket cost to your employer will be.

Realistically, securing a twelve-week paid leave from a small company is no small feat. Your boss is doing the math, thinking about how he or she can't possibly afford to pay you for work you aren't doing (while possibly also needing to hire someone else to fill in). The reality, though, is that a twelve-week paid maternity leave is the *exact same* in dollar figures as a 25 percent retention bonus, which companies readily pay when they are invested in an employee.

And that's what paid parental leave is: both an investment in employees and an investment in a company's future. When huge multinational companies (like Google and Vodafone) looked at the data, they concluded that a generous maternity leave package was worth the cost. Those companies' CEOs are accountable to shareholders, so any decisions they're making are informed by analysis of return on investment. If they value the ROI, your smaller employer might too.

So now that we've covered the basics of maternity leave, let's move on to the next step: talking to your colleagues and developing a coverage plan. For that, read on.

WORTH REMEMBERING

- Read your employee handbook to learn what you can about your company's maternity policy and short-term disability coverage.
- Invest in your personal network: get proactive about getting out and meeting with people while you can still do so without a babysitter, and track those relationships in a spreadsheet or database.
- Identify mentors and peers in your company or industry who have recently had a baby, and start building relationships with them.
- Get your successes down on paper, ideally in conjunction with a conversation with your boss about where your career is going.
- Have a thorough conversation with HR about the logistics of your leave. (You can find a printable list of questions at herestheplanbook.com.)
- Sit down with your boss to have an initial talk about your pregnancy and leave. Plan to talk again in a few months to get really specific about the details.

CHAPTER 2

PUTTING YOUR PLAN INTO ACTION:
PREPARING FOR YOUR LEAVE

After you've had an opportunity to reflect on what you want from your leave—and how that fits into your company's policy and culture—your next big step is developing a coverage plan for your absence. This plan is as much for your manager and colleagues as it is for yourself. I promise: the more you plan and put on paper, the smoother it will go for everyone. But first, you need to share the news.

WHEN AND HOW TO ANNOUNCE YOUR PREGNANCY AT WORK

The first question to consider about announcing your pregnancy in the office is when to tell your boss. Here's the short answer: because the risk of miscarriage is so high, women are encouraged to wait until they're into the second trimester before announcing their pregnancy. But there are other reasons to wait as well.

One of my friends actively hid her pregnancy until she hit the six-month mark. When I told her she didn't even look pregnant, she wryly answered, "That's the point," crediting her growing wardrobe of tunics and leggings. She had just started in a new job, and one of her first to-do's was to hire a direct report. She was concerned that if she disclosed her pregnancy before she made that hire, she would be pressured to hire someone who was potentially overqualified for the role. She recognized that there was some insecurity in that logic, but she wanted to bring someone on who would feel capable but still very challenged. She explained, "I didn't want the person we hired to feel stifled when I came back. I wanted her to be happy to see me, rather than jostling for position on the team."

> "Pregnant women are doing you a favor. If you have an employee whose mother has a stroke, she's not going to give you four months' notice that she's going to need to take time off."
> —CYNTHIA CALVERT, PRESIDENT OF WORKFORCE 21C

Most women talk to their employers early in their second trimester; 45 percent told me that they talked to their boss in the 12-to-14-week range. I was surprised to find that 25 percent told their employers by 12 weeks and 95 percent had shared the news by the time they hit 20 weeks. And while many felt a sense of obligation to give their teams as much time as possible to prepare, remember: your pregnancy affords far more advance notice than any other reason an employee might need to take leave, like having your gallbladder removed or caring for a sick parent. Having a huge buffer of planning time is helpful, but it's not necessary.

Sharing Your Pregnancy: What Can Go Wrong

There's this idea out there that pregnant women are a "protected class." Though that is technically true, it's also incredibly dangerous. In researching this book, I heard women say things like, "Well, I knew my job was safe because I was pregnant," or, "They have to hold my job for twelve weeks." Both of these statements are unfortunately false. If you're an at-will employee (and most employees are), your employer can terminate your employment at any time without any specific reason, so long as it is not for an illegal reason like discrimination. (And if it is discrimination, you have to be able to prove it.) The FMLA offers twelve weeks of "job-protected" leave—during which your employer can't fill your job with someone else—but there's nothing to stop them from eliminating your job.

The sad reality is that, while there are anti-discrimination laws on the books, it is hard to prove that the termination of your employment was related to your pregnancy. A lawyer will tell you it's nowhere near as simple as "I was pregnant, I was laid off, therefore I was laid off because I was pregnant." A half-dozen of the women I spoke with for this book were let go during pregnancy or soon after returning from leave. And note that I wasn't seeking out women who'd had a complicated (or outright bad) experience: my criterion was simply interviewees who'd achieved some measure of professional success and had at least one child under the age of five.

"I had only been at my company for six months when I announced I was pregnant," one marketing director for a global beauty brand told me. Twelve weeks was the most leave she could get approved, despite being in a female-dominated industry—or maybe *because* she was in a female-dominated industry. "There was always someone going out on maternity leave," she explained, "always." It was such a revolving door that there was an HR specialist specifically assigned to managing maternity leave and return.

She was urged to come back at ten weeks, despite her having indicated she would be taking the full twelve weeks she was eligible for. Reluctantly, she returned at ten weeks—only to be laid off a couple of months later. "They called it a 'restructuring,'" she told me, convinced they'd brought her back early just so they could get a full download of her role and responsibilities. She was replaced by a man at her same level. But she didn't pursue legal action, explaining, "I didn't want to be blacklisted in the industry. Everyone knows everyone in beauty, and no one wants to be the troublemaker."

In hindsight, she wonders if an industry with fewer women would have been more welcoming, as ironic as that sounds. "My company didn't need diversity," she said, "in the way a financial services company does. They don't have to be as accommodating, because there are so many other women who want those jobs."

Create a Paper Trail

One way to start protecting yourself is to establish a paper trail that showcases your exemplary performance. (This is very different from a paper trail demonstrating bias toward you; more on that in Chapter 4: Family Responsibilities Discrimination and Pregnancy Discrimination.) This trail is celebratory; it won't depress you or make you paranoid the way a discrimination log might. This is an exercise you should be doing regularly in your career regardless of whether you're pregnant, as it will help you in your next performance review, résumé update, negotiation, or job interview. You'll have at your fingertips a pile of great evidence of your excellent performance and accomplishments.

Formalized performance reviews are a good place to start. If you don't have a copy of your most recent one, ask your HR team. You can explain that you don't have a copy and want to make sure you're really thinking through and addressing the growth areas that you discussed with your manager.

If it's been more than six months, consider asking for an interim review—even before you share the news of your pregnancy in the office. You'll want to get down on paper, independent of your impending maternity leave, that you are an outstanding employee who has tremendous potential. It's not uncommon for employees to ask for a midyear review; you could position it in terms like: "I was looking over the notes from my last review, and I've been really focused on XYZ. I would love to get your feedback on how that's going." If you haven't been at the company very long, ask for an early review, saying something like: "I'm someone who likes a lot of feedback, and I would love to sit down with you to talk about how things have been going."

In this conversation, while you want to uncover priorities that you should be working on, you're *specifically* looking for indications that you're doing your job effectively. Essentially, you want recent documentation that you're a valuable employee. You should prep for this conversation thoroughly: prepare notes listing all your responsibilities, and jot down a few of your big wins so you can readily reference them. One woman I talked to keeps an email folder where she files any accolades she's received from colleagues, and throughout the year she keeps a running list of accomplishments and successful projects.

In the meeting, take copious notes. Type them up afterward, save them for yourself (both on your work computer and in your personal email so you can access them later), and sum them up in a short email to your boss.

In this book's introduction I mentioned how, a couple of weeks before I announced I was pregnant, I had a check-in meeting with a managing director in my firm, who lauded my performance and told me he saw a great future with me. The conversation was casual and friendly, and it never occurred to me to try to document it. Almost a year later, I found myself in mediation with my former company and wished I'd had that written documentation.

Here's the thank-you note I *should* have written right after that meeting:

Dear [Name],

I appreciate your telling me that [specify here the praise you received]. As I shared when I interviewed with you, I love to roll up my sleeves right away, so it's been really exciting to start tapping into the relationships I built with business leaders over my career. The progress I've seen with [big prospective client] has been especially encouraging, and I truly appreciate that the firm recognizes the opportunity here to bring in a heavy-hitting client. Having [the CEO and CFO] join the meeting I arranged at the office made a huge impression.

I'm also personally grateful for the confidence you have signaled in me; I'll be doing everything I can to meet your expectation that I'll be the big success story from my MBA class.

—Allyson

This letter outlines what I bring to the table (a great network) and why he hired me (I'm a go-getter), and it includes a representative example of something I've accomplished (bringing in a client with billion-dollar potential). It also reinforces—with a date stamp, since it comes via email—that we just had a conversation about how he sees great potential in me, as well as specifying exactly what praise I received.

Tailor this basic framework to fit the conversation you have. If you got some constructive criticism, acknowledge it and explain how you'll address it. For example: "Thank you for the feedback that I could be more assertive. You'll be seeing me speak up more frequently in meetings in the coming months." And then *do it*, and reinforce that you've done it with another email in a few months, including specific examples. "As you've seen over the past few months, I've been taking a more active leadership role in division-wide meetings. I've gotten great feedback from [colleagues' names] on [example presentation]. Thank you again for encouraging me."

Just to cover your bases: BCC your personal email address on these types of communications. And keep in mind, this is the opposite of what one lawyer framed to me as a "paranoia diary": it's a written record of the value you bring to the table, and it's accessible to you way down the road because it lives in your personal email. (It couldn't hurt to print and archive these emails as well, or back them up on the cloud. Just be sure you're not violating company policy in doing so.)

Again, these are all tactics you can and should be employing throughout your career, regardless of whether you're pregnant—but they're especially important when you are. As egalitarian and feminist as your employer may be, people can have hang-ups about pregnancy and new parenthood. Put your accomplishments in writing, and then put them in the hands of the people who have decision-making power over your career.

How NOT to Tell Your Boss

Several of the women I talked to had to "come out" earlier than they had planned or wanted to because of social obligations—specifically, the unwritten obligation to drink socially with your colleagues. An investor told me, "I announced at the four-month mark, though I wanted to wait longer, because we were all heading to a conference. I needed to tell them before we left, because it was typically a big drinking thing." Another was outed at a closing dinner by a tipsy colleague who noticed she'd declined wine. "You're not pregnant, *are you?*" the colleague asked. Though she was just eight weeks along, she felt pressured to come clean.

But today her advice to women is to "get comfortable with being evasive" if it isn't yet the right time to talk about your pregnancy at the office. "Run through the possible scenarios in which some nosy person might ask if you're pregnant, and have an answer ready." If you're at that team dinner and the only one not drinking the celebratory champagne, explain that you're on a diet or gave up alcohol because you're training for a half-marathon. Tell them you're taking antibiotics; complain about a headache from overindulging the night before. Practice saying these things out loud in front of a mirror. Though that may sound ridiculous, you need to ensure you don't look sheepish or shifty. Another tactic in the drinking setting: sneak up to the bar and order something that *looks* like a cocktail. At my holiday office party, any onlooker would have assumed my seltzer with lime was a vodka and soda.

If you often come in late or have a lot of doctors' appointments, say you've been ill: "I'm dealing with some health issues. Everything is okay, but I've had a lot of doctor's appointments." One woman, who works sixty miles from home, shared how she found an OB/GYN close to her office so she could go to the early appointments without anyone getting clued in. After she shared the news at work, she switched to a doctor and hospital closer to her house.

Later, you can say, "It was too early to know for sure," or, "We needed to wait on some test results." You're not hiding something; you're protecting your privacy. In short, if you're not ready to talk about your pregnancy, be prepared to redirect any probes into your personal health.

How to Tell Your Boss

I'm personally a fan of the "no big deal" approach to sharing the news of a pregnancy: while personally it's exciting and exhilarating news, from a professional standpoint it's no different from your colleague leaving for a stretch after ACL surgery.

Lynn Perkins, founder of UrbanSitter, was terrified to tell her boss at a hotel chain about her first pregnancy, partly because he was younger, single, and had never expressed interest in children. She finally built up enough courage for the conversation, warning him, "There's something I need to tell you. I don't know how you're going to take this news, but I'm pregnant with twins." She watched relief wash over his face as he said: "I thought you were going to tell me you're quitting!"

Marisa Ricciardi, then a senior executive at NYSE Euronext, included an agenda item called "personal update" as a bullet in her regular check-in with her CEO. "We went through nine items in a status meeting, and when we got to the tenth, I just said, 'I'm going to be a mom.'" She was intentional in not setting a separate meeting; she wanted it to be business as usual. None of her conversations about her pregnancy was *just* about her pregnancy; she made it a nonissue by folding it into other discussions.

I took a similar approach with investors in weeSpring. I agonized over broaching it, worried that they'd be concerned the company would sink without me at the helm. But I bucked up some courage and included a short note at the bottom of a broader investor update. "And lastly," I wrote, "some good news. We'll be welcoming another Downey in June (a girl!), so we'll be in an *even better* place to build value with weeSpring for parents beyond their first child." And while it wasn't conscious at the time, I noticed later that I hadn't used the word "baby," "pregnant," or "maternity."

One of my friends, a venture capitalist, told her partners in one of their regular investment review meetings. She said she was pregnant, but then told them that she wanted to let the news sink in for a few weeks before actually talking logistics. "It was like a bomb went off in the room," she said. "Everyone was expecting it, but no one wanted to hear it." She was already prepared for a negotiation, but that wait time gave her partners some time to accept that they'd need to step up in her absence.

One entertainment executive received an unexpected promotion when she was called into a routine meeting with her boss, which sent the wheels spinning in her head about announcing her pregnancy. She told him how excited she was and riffed a bit about short-term priorities before adding, "Since we're having this career talk, you should know I'm pregnant."

"He didn't say 'Congratulations.' He didn't say, 'That's wonderful.' He didn't say, 'How could you!'" After a few beats, he finally said, "HR told me I should not say anything in these moments." Though it was awkward and uncomfortable, they wrapped up the meeting and she jumped into her role. And she didn't dwell on his odd reaction: "I was on the clock to start hiring people and on-boarding them before I needed to take leave."

Only 3 percent of the more than two thousand women I surveyed reported a negative response to their announcements. In the overwhelming majority of cases, their managers were happy for them—even overjoyed. One woman told me her manager started jumping up and down in the office.

When one of my friends told her boss she was pregnant, he excitedly steered the conversation into the logistics of parental leave. His wife was due two months before she was, and he planned to take his paternity leave. "He wanted parents on the team to use their leave," she told me. "It was a really supportive culture."

But regardless of how positive a response you receive, there may be a different interior monologue roiling under the surface. Your supervisor is human, and she's likely to have a human reaction, most likely: "What's this going to mean for *me*?" Specifically, she's probably wondering:

- How long will she be gone?
- How are we going to do what we need to do without her?
- Is she really going to come back?

You can manage this situation by squashing those questions and concerns and proactively answering them. For the first two questions, you can buy yourself some time by acknowledging them and stating that you'll circle back with a plan shortly. For example: "I have some initial thoughts on a coverage plan for my absence, and I would like to sit down in a week to discuss them."

Whether she's aware of it or not, your supervisor has biases about pregnant women, and you can address those biases without needing to acknowledge them as concerns. Say something like, "I appreciate how happy you are for me, and I want you to know how committed I am to my job and this company." Your boss needs to hear that you're not going to leave her in the lurch. This is something you can and should interject every few months, even after you return from leave. "Talk in three-month chunks," one executive coach advised. "Remind your manager how temporary this phase is by saying things like, 'At three months, I'll be back in the office,' or 'At six months, I'll be in the office four days and working from home one day.' Don't phrase any of these things as an accommodation." Just state them as the plan.

And speak up early and often about the types of assignments and work you would like. If you're still able to travel, be explicit in stating that. If you want to take on a big project before the baby is due, say so. So much of the discrimination women face is what attorney Cynthia Calvert calls "benevolent discrimination." Your manager doesn't want to burden you, or believes it would be hard on you to be on your feet at a trade show for four days. But there's a big problem in this kind of "generosity." Your overly considerate manager can rob you of valuable experiences you need to get promoted. Mitigate that by clearly expressing what you want.

Complicating that benevolent discrimination is the general (and often overwhelming) fear of a lawsuit. According to Calvert, who consults for major corporations, many supervisors don't understand the laws around pregnancy protections. Your direct manager may not broach with you a plan for your departure and return, perhaps because he or she doesn't know what's required or is worried about a possible FMLA violation. *You have to be proactive.*

Jennifer Dulski, now the president and COO of Change.org, was at Yahoo when she had both of her children. A few weeks into her leave after having her second baby, a senior manager told her he was about to launch a big new project, and he'd heard from everyone that she'd be a huge asset to the team. But in order to be staffed on this project, she would need to come back to work right away. He was clear that the ball was in her court, and she didn't have to cut short her maternity leave if she didn't want to, but he wanted her to have the opportunity to make the choice herself. "A lot of people may have been offended or upset by a call like that," she said. "But I wound up saying 'yes,' and I worked out an arrangement that allowed me to work from home a few days a week."

This is really murky territory, because most employers don't want to inadvertently rush someone back into work. But it would be wise to think now about how you'd feel if you received that call—and if it's a call you'd welcome, tell your supervisor. Roll it into other conversations you're having about the kind of work you want to do before you leave, as well as the types of things you'd like to dive into when you're back. Say, "I want you to know that if any big opportunities come up, I would like to be considered for them, even if it seems like they may interfere with my leave." Dulski concurs, having been on both sides of the table: "Managers aren't mind readers," she said. "Every individual will be different, so you have to speak up."

These conversations with your manager are another opportunity to get down in writing how valuable you are to the company. Your coverage plan is basically your job description, and you can use it both to be crystal clear about your responsibilities and to ensure they're there for you when you return. You also can highlight your successes: "As you know, Client X relies heavily on me since we delivered [huge win], but I will start getting [colleague] up to speed on their account to steward them until my return." One woman told me, "Writing everything down helped alleviate my stress, but it also helped me realize how much I do in a workday." She used her conversation with her manager to highlight how much responsibility she had taken on, and she believes it elevated her profile. (You can find stories from women who created successful coverage plans later in this chapter.)

When to Tell Your Colleagues and Other Stakeholders

You also need a plan for telling other professional stakeholders, because these conversations can be even more critical to your success than the one you have with your boss. For colleagues inside the company, they'll in many cases be the ones covering your job—and taking on a significant amount of new (and potentially burdensome) responsibility in your absence.

One woman I talked to, concerned she'd be treated differently by her colleagues, delayed telling them for as long as possible, though she did tell her boss early on. And while she was careful to still give them enough notice, she appreciated having "less time that they were viewing me as a walking pumpkin about to give birth."

While your boss may have been conditioned to understand that he can't (or at least shouldn't) treat you differently because you're pregnant, your colleagues might not feel that kind of professional responsibility. It may be a little cynical to say this, but your peers in the office may be wondering how much of your job they'll be expected to shoulder, and whether you're really coming back.

You may want to wait until you have a good sense of your coverage plan before your initial conversation; being proactive about communicating exactly when you'll be out and who will be taking on what spares them having to wonder and worry. You'll also want to explain (and this goes for every conversation you have about your pregnancy at the office) that you want to be the one to share the news with others. One woman warned of "professional sabotage," where a colleague tells a higher-up that you're pregnant before you have the chance to.

Another thing to consider: the inferences your colleagues are making from your casual mentions of your baby. A marketing director told me that she regretted talking as much as she did about her pregnancy and plans for her baby; in hindsight, she thinks she may have been sending an inadvertent signal that she was wholly focused on her pregnancy and new status as a mother, and not so focused on returning to her job.

Externally, the stakes can be even higher when telling clients you need to retain, investors you need to keep happy, and partners who rely on you. Every woman I talked to who had external stakeholders had a clear coverage plan in place before she shared the news. For example: this is how long I will be gone, this is what I'll be taking care of before I leave, this is who will be your go-to while I'm out, and this is how you can reach me in an emergency. (I talk more about this in the "Making Your Plan" section coming up.)

Many women spent months transitioning their colleagues into the relationship, sometimes even starting before the clients knew they were pregnant. They would bring a colleague into meetings, CC her on emails, and have her join conference calls so the clients would have ample time to get comfortable with her and confident that they'd be well covered.

Jennifer Hill was a practicing attorney at a law firm when she had her first baby. A few months before she left, she reached out to clients to let them know she'd be leaving. For some, she immediately started looping in a colleague on emails; for others, she scheduled a "hand-off" call for two weeks before she was leaving. The clients liked that they'd been introduced to someone she'd handpicked to cover for her. "A lot of them sent me a baby gift," she said, which she took as an indication they were satisfied with how she'd handled the transition.

If you're meeting someone for the first time, though, consider waiting to discuss your pregnancy until you've established a relationship. Caitlin MacGregor, the CEO of Plum, was six months pregnant when she embarked on a fundraising round for her company. She never referenced her pregnancy until after her initial meeting, and she was pleasantly surprised to find that she could camouflage her belly most of the time. "I'd wear a black top and black maxi skirt, with a bright cardigan and necklace," she said. When she walked into the room, she'd shake the person's hand and then sit down behind a table. If they expressed serious interest, she'd then mention that she would be out of the office for six weeks during their slowest months, but she'd still be online. "They were usually shocked that they hadn't noticed I was pregnant," she told me. "It's personal. I don't talk about my four-year-old when I start a meeting or bring him along with me. I didn't want my unborn child to be the first thing someone noticed about me."

THE UNPLEASANT REALITIES OF BEING PREGNANT IN AN OFFICE

It's easier said than done to wait months to explain to your colleagues why you're dragging all of the time, or rushing off to the bathroom whenever someone wearing heavy cologne walks by. My friend Tracy lived in perpetual fear that someone would walk into the bathroom while she was in there barfing. "I worried they'd think I was bulimic." She explained it as "a hangover that doesn't feel better as the day goes on."

She told me she fell asleep at her desk more than once; she'd wake up not knowing how much time had gone by, but she had some cover in that everyone worked incredibly long hours. "Someone would have just thought I'd been working really hard!" But despite feeling that bone-crushing tiredness and constant nausea, she never talked about it. "You never want to be the complainer. I didn't want to stand out or make it seem like I had a disability." But pregnancy is a very, very physical thing. She'd expected she'd be one of the women who go on an eight-mile run while pregnant, but that was a complete impossibility. The emotions brought on by hormones didn't help. "I felt like a failure," Tracy shared.

Those hormones are serious business. In the early months of pregnancy, your progesterone spikes as high as one hundred times normal levels. In her book *The Female Brain*, Dr. Louann Brizendine compares the sedating effects of progesterone to those of Valium, noting how the "tranquilizing effect of progesterone and also high estrogen help protect against stress hormones during pregnancy."[4] So there's a *very good reason* you're exhausted. Meanwhile, your stress hormones (like cortisol) are steadily climbing. "Their impact is to make a pregnant woman vigilant about her safety, nutrition, and surroundings, and less attuned to other kinds of tasks, such as making conference calls and organizing her schedule."

One woman I talked to transitioned out of one high-profile tech job into another and got pregnant three months later. She waited until the end of her first trimester to tell her boss, but that entire time she felt disingenuous for concealing—or, rather, not revealing—her pregnancy. "I'd read somewhere that you're not supposed to say anything earlier than that, so I waited."

> **"I couldn't lean in. If I wasn't leaning over a trash can, it was a great day."**
> —MARIA SEIDMAN, CEO AND COFOUNDER OF YAPP

But meanwhile, she was getting violently ill and was more tired than she'd ever been in her life. "Some days I felt like I couldn't even get out of bed, but I forced myself to." She managed that exhaustion by getting more selective about the meetings she'd take. Previously, she was getting coffee or drinks with anyone she thought she could potentially recruit to join the new company, but after getting hit with serious pregnancy fatigue, she shifted to a process that was more rigorous for the candidates but less demanding for her. She started doing video calls instead of face-to-face meetings, and it made a huge difference.

Around the time she hit the 12-week mark, the company CEO joked to her, "You better not get pregnant!" He meant it lightly, and she interpreted it as expressing how valuable she was to the team. Still, her stomach dropped. "I'm a very open and transparent person. When he said that, it made me feel like I'd been keeping a secret from him." So she told him the next day; he was kind and supportive, and he put the ball in her court to figure out a maternity leave policy for the company.

You may be reluctant to (in one woman's words) "admit weakness" by asking for accommodations like flexible working hours, but small changes like starting an hour later or leaving an hour earlier can be a make-or-break scenario. I personally could not get anywhere before 9:30 AM during my pregnancy, because the process of getting dressed involved an ungodly number of breaks so I could sit down and

LOOKING GOOD, FEELING GOOD

In a 2012 study, two researchers identified a concept they called "enclothed cognition": the idea that what you wear impacts how you think. They ran an experiment in which they dressed random participants in lab coats, then compared their performance of attention-related tasks with that of individuals who hadn't been given anything special to wear. The lab-coat wearers significantly outperformed their peers.[5]

Courtney Klein is the founder of Storq, which sends you a bundle of simple maternity fashion basics that you can integrate with your "regular" wardrobe. "Professional women have a different set of wants and needs than they did a few decades ago," she said. "Their pregnancies are only one aspect of their lives and how they want to define themselves." She developed what she calls "your base layer": soft, stretchy staples that you can still look like yourself in. "You're a mother and ____," she said "not just a mother." She wanted to make pregnancy feel like less of a compromise, and help women feel a little more human.

She advised *not* overhauling your wardrobe for your pregnancy; not only is doing so expensive, it can be an even bigger dead giveaway in the office than your growing belly. "Blazers are especially useful," she said, because you already have them in your closet, they will always fit, and they camouflage or accentuate your "bump," depending on what stage of pregnancy you're in. Cardigans, chunky jewelry, and cute (and comfortable) shoes are all things you'll be able to wear post-pregnancy as well, in that awkward stage when you don't yet fit back in your regular clothes. "There's this urge to burn your maternity clothes after pregnancy," Courtney said, "but you're still stuck with them for a little while, so there's value in investing in pieces that you can feel confident in."

focus on not throwing up. But I never would have admitted to anyone that was why I wouldn't set breakfast meetings.

When you're in the office, stock your desk with snacks; they'll help keep the nausea at bay. One woman advised keeping a pillow stashed away so you can squeeze a quick nap in between meetings; even if you can't swing a nap, you'll appreciate having it there for lower back support at your desk chair.

And unless you're in a job that sticks to a rigid schedule (like a standing 8:30 AM meeting), you might not have to get specific. Try to ask without offering an explanation. For example:

- "I'd like to adjust my hours to start at 10:00 AM for the next couple of months, though I'll be on email before then and will make up the time in the evening."
- "I'd like to leave at 4:00 PM, but I will be back online at 8:00 PM."
- "I'd like to work from home on Wednesdays."

Instead of focusing on why you need this, explain how nothing in practical terms will change. Assure your boss that your job is still going to get done, and put an end date on the request if you think you'll need it for only a finite period. You can always go back and say, "The flexibility to work from home one day a week has been great for me and the project I'm working on. I've been able to get ahead on XYZ because I have fewer interruptions during the day. I'd love to continue doing it." One attorney told me, "I proved while pregnant that I was responsible enough to work an adjusted schedule, so it was really a nonissue when I wanted the same flexibility after my baby was born."

SETTING PRIORITIES

I can't emphasize this enough: this is the time to double down on your commitment to your professional life—not necessarily in hours spent or energy expended, but in laying the groundwork for your post-baby return (and success!), and shoring up your professional network. The latter is something that's ignored by too many women.

When I was in my twenties, I was fortunate to find a mentor in Kathy Wylde, the CEO for Partnership for New York City, a nonprofit that aligns the political and governmental interests of the biggest corporations in the city, which also happen to be some of the biggest corporations in the world. She was in daily communication with, and highly respected by, the people I've always thought of as the masters of the universe: marquee names that you'd recognize if you picked up *The Wall Street Journal* even just once a month. One time she and I got to talking about the spectacular fall (from "Acme") of a top female executive, whom we'll call Jill. "Where Jill went wrong," Kathy told me, "was in not building relationships outside Acme." She went on to explain that when she has looked at and worked with successful men—and her advisory board is stacked with dozens of them—she has noticed that they have a wide reach across companies and industries. They seek out professional organizations that allow them to network broadly, and they strategically cultivate and maintain relationships with influencers at other companies. So when there's a major leadership change (bringing along with it an overthrow of the current regime) or your company shifts its priorities—or there's a bad quarter and layoffs are on the horizon—they already have a communication channel open elsewhere. They get a drink with their friend at a competitor and say, "So I'm thinking about making a change. What does the landscape look like right now at ____?"

Women don't set up these networks for themselves as strategically and relentlessly as men do. If women play politics, they're focused on doing so inside their own firm. If you come back from maternity leave and your division head has been replaced by someone who isn't particularly sympathetic to the challenges of working parents, you need a broader safety net than the one you'll find by trying to transfer to another division.

Just as you'll need a roster of backup babysitters (more on that in Chapter 6: Hiring a Caregiver), you'll need a roster of backup employers. It may sound glib, but as I mentioned before, there are no guarantees when it comes to pregnancy protections, and you're entering into a life phase when your financial stability means more than ever before.

Early on in my career I believed professional success was all about merit and hard work. It's taken me more than fifteen years to figure out that I was wrong—and that maximizing your connections isn't nepotism, it's efficiency. In many cases, professional opportunities don't even get posted: they're filled through internal channels (though not necessarily with internal candidates) and many great positions are won by being in the right place at the right time.

And while some equate networking with job hunting, note that establishing the kind of rapport that will give someone confidence in referring you takes time, often spent at casual after-work drinks or early-morning breakfasts. But in a few months, finding that time will require caregiver juggling, and your first pregnancy is one of the last windows of time in which scheduling networking meetings is relatively uncomplicated.

Once you are a parent, you won't have time to be everywhere at once, but you can achieve a similar outcome by having a broad swath of people who are your personal and professional allies, all looking out for you. Building an influential network is not rocket science, but it takes a fair amount of grunt work and a little insight into what motivates people.

First, trying to meet someone "quality" at a networking event is the equivalent of going to a bar to find a boyfriend. They're both mostly full of people you don't want to or need to meet—and you don't have time for that anymore. Get warm intros from your friends to get to know interesting people; write up an email friends can easily forward to their college classmates, the head of marketing at Macy's, or their cousin's ex-girlfriend who happens to be the director of HR at Procter & Gamble. The email should give a little bit of personal

TIME, MONEY, AND BABY GADGETS

Because of the time I've spent building weeSpring, I'm uniquely aware of just how much time pregnant women spend on "preparing" for their baby: they stress about every item of baby gear they may or may not need, and they nest like crazy because there's a hormonal imperative to do so.

I say all this as someone who closely monitors the shopping and researching habits of parents (it's my job to do so!) but also as someone who spent hours and hours reading reviews of car seats. And I have good news: your baby will be okay with the simple basics, and you don't have to have every single thing purchased and arranged in the nursery before you go into labor. One adoptive mom told me, "I showed up at the hospital with a car seat and some onesies. They gave us diapers there, and we bought everything else once we got home."

Other cultures understand this and try to reduce the burden on new parents: since the 1930s, Finland has sent a box of simple necessities to expecting mothers, including some basic baby clothes, cloth diapers, little hats, and nursing pads. The box it comes in doubles as a crib; *that's* how simple a baby's needs are in those early months.

But keeping your career alive (and thriving) is more complex. So back away from the baby registry—or at least, the obsessive research about what to put on your baby registry. If people want to know what you need—and you're not sure yet—ask for gift certificates that you'll be able to use for diapers or other gear you'll discover as your baby grows. If you later realize you need a baby swing because you've got a colicky newborn on your hands, you can use the gift certificates then—*or* you can get a hand-me-down from a friend.

The cost of diapers is no joke: families spend thousands of dollars on diapers (BabyCenter estimates $72 a month for

→

disposable)—and that's just a small fraction of your overall spending on baby gear. And your spending on baby gear is in turn a tiny fraction of what you'll spend on childcare.

For many people, this goes without saying, but be frugal when you can. Borrow from friends, especially for things that babies outgrow quickly, and remind yourself that there is *no* correlation between the price of your crib and how much you love your baby. Remember: Finns tuck their newborns into cardboard-box cribs, and Finnish teenagers have scored highest *in the world* on the PISA (Program for International Student Assessment) scholarly aptitude test.

I don't want to be unrealistic here: you're having a *baby*! It's exciting and scary and overwhelming, and you need to afford yourself some time to dream—and worry, within reason—about how your life is going to change.

So when you're doing your deep research on the "best" baby products, I hope you'll internalize the phrase that's become my mantra: There's no single "best" when it comes to baby products, just what's best for your family. And for some families, best will be the $100 crib from IKEA that allows them to save a few hundred dollars in a rainy day fund or take an extra couple days of maternity leave.

background on you, explain what you're looking for, and specifically outline what's in it for them. (That last part is the most important and most often overlooked: do *not* ask to pick someone's brain. These people are busy, and they need a good reason to take time out of their schedules to talk with you.)

Here's an example:

> *I noticed on LinkedIn that you're connected to [name of the person you want to meet], and I was wondering if you know her well enough to make an introduction.*
>
> *As you might be aware, I've been working to build [your company's] digital marketing strategy, and I would love to get [name]'s insight into how they've managed their cross-promotional partnerships with brands. We've made great inroads with other retailers and helped in driving traffic to them, so hopefully it could be a beneficial relationship to her, too.*

You need to have a real reason to ask for the meeting or call, but it doesn't have to be 100 percent concrete—nor does it have to be professional. Find some commonality, and build from there. It's even easier if you're asking someone close to you for the introduction, as you could have her say something as simple as, "I wanted to introduce you to my friend because you're both hard-charging women in real estate who are expecting babies," or, "Your name came up the other day when I was talking to my friend [your name], and I realized I've never introduced you."

Rinse and repeat.

One of the best pieces of personal advice I can offer is to find a systematic way to keep track of those relationships: use a Google spreadsheet, a tool like Streak, or even the "relationship" tab on your LinkedIn connections to track when you've met with someone, how you know them, and anything else you may not have space to store in your brain. (That brain capacity is changing rapidly; more on that in Chapter 7: Returning to Work.) When you need to tap into those connections, you shouldn't spend time and energy trying to remember whom you know at Procter & Gamble—and you won't have to, if you invest in a system now.

MAKING YOUR PLAN

It's time to dig into the nitty-gritty of how your job will get done in your absence, from how accessible you want to be to who will be taking on what. There's a menu of options for pretty much every decision you'll be making, and each selection has its own benefits and drawbacks. Much like every other aspect of your pregnancy and leave (and ultimately, parenting), there is no single right answer.

Will you have some kind of meeting in which you run through the basics? Are you going to have one-on-one conversations with everyone? Would an email outlining everything be enough? What will your out-of-office response say? Do you want to be copied on all email correspondence while you're gone? (If so, you might return to an avalanche of emails, many of which would have been long since resolved.)

A teacher found that her internal colleagues were much more respectful of her leave than people who were external: parents simply ignored her out-of-office auto-reply and tried to reach her on her cell phone. But if you're worried about internal colleagues, designating a gatekeeper can help: a sole person who determines if and when it is really necessary to reach you. That gatekeeper can also elevate anything to your attention that's coming from someone outside your organization. One woman advised making these boundaries tougher than you think you'll need them to be, since that first outreach from the office can be like a crack in a dam. (This approach also gives you an opportunity to underpromise and overdeliver.)

A number of women described the documents they created to guide their colleagues in their absence: some were physical binders, others were stored on the cloud with lots of embedded hyperlinks.

They all emphasized how important it is to put everything in writing: who to consult for what, how to do XYZ, what needs to happen when, etc. One woman started copying her boss on all emails three months before her due date, a strategy that could be applied to anyone covering for you. You can also set up calendar reminders for yourself on your smartphone for anything that you want to do or need to do personally.

In creating these documents you're also building a written record of what your roles and responsibilities were prior to your leave. An advertising executive learned upon return from maternity leave that her position was being eliminated; the agency soon hired a male who essentially did her same job. Needless to say, she laments not putting everything in writing.

Another thing to reflect on: what decisions are you comfortable delegating, and when do you want to be consulted? It can be spectacularly hard to let go, especially when you're the only one with the institutional knowledge and experience to steer the ship. One woman, newly named CEO of a large nonprofit organization, told me: "My predecessor could completely unplug for two weeks with no access to his phone, and nothing would go wrong, because I was there. He literally could go to Antarctica—and did." But because she was so new to the role, she hadn't had time to groom a second-in-command, and she felt the stakes were too high not to weigh in. She'd just taken on this big job—her dream job—and if anything fell apart in her absence, it could jeopardize that. But on the other side, she'd tried for *seven years* to get pregnant, and she was hungry for that blissful, immersive bonding time with her baby. She summed up what so many women grapple with: "When I was working, I was angry, and when I wasn't, I was worried."

Options for Time Away

The two ends of the spectrum on maternity leave are what I like to call "full blackout" (whereby you're completely offline and unreachable except in case of true, dire emergency) and staying 100 percent online (plugged in to your office via the various devices you rely on).

As for the plugged-in approach: one woman told me matter-of-factly that she worked during her entire maternity leave(s), albeit remotely. "I wanted to stay on top of the projects I cared about," she said. She was also reluctant to completely turn over her work to junior team members because she wanted to be able to seamlessly ramp up again—even though her company and managers would have been fine with her disengaging for a few months. She never even put up an out-of-office message.

The truth, though, is that for the majority of high-achieving, career-oriented women, maternity leave falls somewhere in between these two extremes. A partner in a venture capital firm had a "partial blackout" plan, which gave her six weeks of uninterrupted, unplugged time with the baby, and then six more weeks in which she was partially engaged, participating in weekly conference calls and keeping up with email. Unfortunately, just two weeks postpartum, one of her portfolio companies hit upon a true, dire emergency—so she held a board meeting in her kitchen while her mother took care of the baby upstairs. Ever focused, she kept it to two hours to fit between breast-feeding sessions.

Many women opted for the partial-engagement side of her plan. Given that the idea of coming back to thousands of unread email messages can be panic-inducing, many occasionally logged on to delete or archive the things that didn't require their response. Others did scheduled check-ins, or in some cases stopped by the office. With my second child, when we were a year and a half into running weeSpring, it simply wasn't an option for me to disengage. I offloaded as much as I could, and then I put up a vague out-of-office message saying I was offline because I'd just had a baby. I was unspecific about a return date, and I directed any urgent questions to my cofounder. The truth, though, was that I checked email regularly, at least a couple of times a day, even in the very beginning. But that out-of-office reply gave me cover on the nonessential emails, allowing me to simply ignore them without being rude.

Be sure to manage expectations—both those of your colleagues and your own. The first months after having a baby are "a tiring time for your brain," as one woman described. "Most likely, there are better solutions for your coworkers than having to depend on an underslept new mother, whether it's an emergency or not."

If you quarterback your duties and projects thoroughly during your pregnancy, you can pull off a "real" maternity leave without even needing an out-of-office auto-response. Early on in her pregnancy, Sara Holoubek, CEO of Luminary Labs, introduced her clients and contacts to the person who'd be taking the reins while she was out, so they had plenty of time to build the relationship. Her team kept a running Google Doc of what was going on so she could stay apprised (on her own schedule), and in their emails to her they utilized subject-line hashtags like #FWYAB (for when you are back) and #IMPT. She could review her email from home without delving into the rabbit hole of things that weren't urgent, and simply forwarded unanticipated external emails for a colleague to reply to on her behalf.

A couple of savvy women tracked and were compensated for the time they spent working in the months they were technically out on leave. A partner at a global communications firm used the billable hours she logged during her leave to take Fridays off after she returned to work full-time. Laura Walsh Boone, an attorney in West Virginia, said: "I think a lot of employers would be willing to do this if women just knew to ask." And one woman who didn't get paid leave negotiated a consulting deal for the time she was out of the office.

Margo Buchanan leads alternative energy investments for a private company. Since no one else there could shoulder all her responsibilities, her company designated someone to take on her responsibilities under the guidance of Margo's roughly five-hours-a-week coaching. She loved it: "I wound up managing my old job, but from a higher level. I was happy to take those calls and have a chance to think about something other than nappies or sleep." And she structured the deal smartly; the first five hours were at a very high hourly rate, because she wanted them to think twice about calling her—and if she was going to take time away from the baby, she needed to be well compensated for it. That rate dropped as she accrued more hours over the week, which kept her from pricing herself out of her job as she progressed further along in her leave.

But full blackout *is* do-able for some. Fran Hauser unplugged completely during her first maternity leave. Prior to leaving she reviewed every major project, assigning it to someone on her team and defining what success looked like. She invested up-front in preparing her direct reports for her absence, and also put together "a massive spreadsheet" for her boss so he'd know who was handling what. Everyone knew how to reach her while she was gone, but no one needed to.

What makes this all the more remarkable is that Fran adopted her children, so she didn't even know that she might be leaving until six weeks prior to her departure. "When you're pregnant, you have ten months to plan. When you're adopting, you don't know what's going to happen. It's a very vulnerable and tenuous situation." Reluctant to share any news before it looked like the adoption was rock-solid (or as rock-solid as adoption can be), she waited until two weeks before the birth mother's due date to tell her colleagues.

But in the weeks prior to that announcement, she was quietly getting organized, reflecting on the major things that would happen while she was gone. "I wanted to set everyone up for success," she told me, so she developed spreadsheets with clear deliverables and goals. With all of those lists and outlines ready before her announcement, when she shared her news, she used her time together with the group to ask them to pull together their own assessments of what was critical. Then, when she met individually with her direct reports, she used her notes to add to what they had prepared. Ultimately, everyone was left with a clear sense of what their three-month goals were.

In her meeting with her boss, she handed over a document that listed each major initiative (like a product launch or companies they were looking to acquire), along with the person who would own that initiative in her absence. She was also open and transparent about her concerns, calling his attention to the two or three areas in which she thought he might need to get involved; she credits some of her success to being candid about these trouble spots.

Her best advice applies to most women planning leave: "The more you can put down on paper for your boss and your direct reports, the more likely you'll be able to disconnect."

Covering Your Bases

"Document, document, document."
—KATHLEEN WARNER, FOUNDING COO OF
STARTUP AMERICA PARTNERSHIP

As I mentioned in chapter 1, your coverage plan is just a (very!) extensive version of your job description. It serves a few purposes:

- It illustrates your value to your employer by laying out all your contributions to the company or organization—as well as showcasing your dedication to the job.
- It provides a road map for your colleagues to carry forward your work in your absence.
- It will ease your reentry, serving as a checklist to help you get up to speed on what you've missed.
- It's a record of your pre-leave responsibilities, should you need to have a conversation with your employer about an unwelcome change in your job.

You'll want to list all of the projects you're currently working on, specify action items, and designate an "owner" for each. Some women created two versions: the one that they shared with their supervisors, and the one that they left for the person or people who'd be carrying out their duties.

When you deliver that plan to your supervisor, consider copying HR on that email. One woman who did so told me, "I wanted to have a record that I'd properly transitioned everything."

The Who, the How, and the When

Ideally, you'll be able to decide who will cover your work in your absence. Jennifer Hill drafted a list of all her clients and responsibilities, proposed an "owner" for each, and delivered it to the partners at her firm. "I just said, 'Here's the plan.'" If you're working in a male-dominated industry, chances are your manager or managers have never had to consider how to execute a transition like this for themselves. "They're focused on whatever fire is burning brightest at that moment," she said.

But even if you're not granted a say in who takes the reins in your absence, don't assume that someone else, like your boss or HR, has coverage lined up for you. I was surprised by how many women described a last-minute scramble to ensure their work continued uninterrupted. Be direct and ask who will fill your role during your leave; if it will be an outsider, find out who will be hiring that person.

Even in the situations where coverage has been lined up or considered, sometimes the person proposed isn't up for the task. A marketing director told me she was appalled by the choices that were floated; another woman was insulted that her boss thought the junior-level people he suggested were capable of doing her job. "It was a wake-up call that he didn't really comprehend the value I brought."

No matter who's covering for you while you're on leave, trust is the bedrock for success: you have to trust that your substitute will be able to execute your responsibilities, and you have to trust that your job will still be yours when you get back—both of which are easier said than done. You've also got to manage expectations—both your own and your team's—about what will realistically get done while you're gone. "I found that my team could finish things that we'd started before I left," one woman shared, "but they weren't able to initiate anything new without me." Be honest with yourself about what needs to go on hold, and then be honest with the people around you.

Among all the women who contributed their experience to this book, five primary "coverage plans" emerged, meaning whether the person covering was over her (her boss), under her (a direct report), lateral (a colleague), outside (a consultant or freelancer), or all over (responsibilities divided amongst the team). As you'd likely expect, there are pros and cons to each.

When your BOSS is stepping in, you know that the person watching over your projects and relationships has the experience and institutional knowledge to handle the big issues—but the smaller tasks and responsibilities might fall through the cracks.

The converse can be true if one of your DIRECT REPORTS steps up: the many smaller details will get handled, but your stand-in may not have the expertise or experience to steer through bigger challenges. When elevating direct reports, you have the opportunity to signal both your investment in your direct reports' professional development *and* your confidence in their ability to rise to the challenge. Several women told me the people they designated were excited to be given the chance to take on leadership responsibilities and interface directly with senior management.

This is where trust is paramount: you don't want to blindly elevate someone into your seat if you think that person could be angling for it. One senior executive from Google returned to a passive-aggressive direct report who, emboldened by her experience over the previous six months, seemed unsatisfied with her newly reduced responsibilities. Fortunately they found her another role elsewhere in the company where she'd have more room to grow, but the situation could have devolved into the direct report undermining the executive.

A LATERAL coverage plan, whereby a peer takes on your responsibilities, puts a competent person in your place. But unless his or her role gets scaled back during this period, your replacement can be left overcommitted, and potentially resentful.

A great solution for that concern is hiring an OUTSIDER, as that person will have full bandwidth. But it can also be time-consuming to recruit, screen, and train that person. One phenomenon—particularly common in industries dominated by thirtysomething women—is the ex-employee who comes back exclusively to cover maternity leaves. She's typically a mother who has opted not to return full-time after having a child, but who engages for one or two twelve-week stints a year. She knows the key players and the culture, and in a lot of instances she's previously done the day-to-day work required. Maybrooks, a flexible job-search engine and career resource for mothers, has a category of job listings called "maternityships." "We created this category so women could post their own jobs," said founder Stacey Delo. "There's a lot of anxiety about stepping away from a job and feeling like no one can do it but you—or that there's someone who would replace you more permanently." Tapping a highly qualified woman who has left the workforce but is looking for project-based work can mitigate that anxiety.

Of all the above plans where an individual other than your boss will be filling your shoes, leave some time for that person to shadow you. One real estate investor allowed two weeks for that person to get up to speed; in the second week, she reversed roles so the temporary hire could actually start doing the job, tapping her for support as needed. Not surprisingly, this approach empowered her temporary replacement with the know-how she needed to cover the role.

TEAM COVERAGE is most common in instances where there's a flat organization, like at a consulting firm, where several people work collaboratively on a single project. For some people on project-based work, a project will wrap up around the time you're slated for leave. It can be a huge relief not to have anything to worry about after your baby has been born, but it also tends to mean you have to scramble to get assigned to something once you return. For a few women this project hunt toward the end of maternity leave caused considerable anxiety, and one found herself shut out entirely. If you can, try to network internally before you leave to lay the groundwork for a new assignment upon your return.

The Unplanned

As I mentioned earlier, while I'd expected to work until I went into labor, I had to leave the office unexpectedly and semi-abruptly at 22 weeks because my doctor advised that I work from home 75 percent of the time. My company was outwardly understanding and supportive, but I still struggled to get access to everything I needed to do my job effectively while working remotely. When my situation worsened, it was recommended I go on bed rest, and I joined the 20 percent of American women whose doctors advise them to reduce their activity during pregnancy.

Pregnancy accommodations, like working from home or with a reduced workload, are still a legal gray area. Recently, though, in a groundbreaking pregnancy accommodations case argued before the Supreme Court, *Young v. UPS*, the court sided with the plaintiff in saying UPS failed to provide appropriate pregnancy accommodations. Though the legal ramifications of that decision are still emerging, it was a significant step forward for pregnant women. (Chapter 4: Family Responsibilities Discrimination and Pregnancy Discrimination discusses discrimination concerns in greater depth.)

Needless to say, the best plan is an early plan—don't wait until week 37 to start drafting it. Start prepping for your absence as soon as you know there will be one, even if it is just a simple checklist of your responsibilities. Then, as you progress in your pregnancy, flesh it out further. Keep this list where you can access it outside the office; if you find yourself unexpectedly bed-bound, you can dash it off to your colleagues. One woman advised having all documents you're actively working on stored on a shared drive that your colleagues can access. Another drafted her "go plan" and kept it on the company server: a document detailing all standard operating procedures for her job as well as all the important notes and contacts her colleagues would need if she had to go out unexpectedly.

More practical to-do's: get a doctor's note detailing what you can and cannot do. These notes are the foundation for any future legal claims, so it is critically important that they be worded precisely and thoughtfully, yet too few doctors know how to frame this language in a way that protects the woman's job. In 2015, the Center for WorkLife Law launched a new resource called Pregnant@Work, offering specific guidance for health care professionals on drafting effective work notes to avoid the pitfalls that can lead to a woman being unnecessarily sent out on leave or fired (pregnantatwork.org).

Talk to your Human Resources team about what telework tools they have in place—or could establish. One woman told her HR team very succinctly: "I want to work as long as possible. You want me to work as long as possible. How can we make this happen?" With resources like VPNs, Dropbox, Skype, and Google Docs, there are countless ways you can stay connected with your office, even just in the short term to arrange for a handover. You'll also want to ask HR about how this time impacts the amount of time you can take after the baby is born.

Remember: it is in your company's best interest to keep you and your baby healthy, particularly if you are covered by your company's health insurance. As one HR executive pointed out, "A day in the NICU [neo-natal intensive care unit] is expensive."

Last, have a direct conversation with your boss about the implications of this early leave. Make sure she (or he) has a copy of your document that explains your coverage plan, and emphasize that you remain as committed as ever to your job. Remember, just as when you're sharing the news of a pregnancy, your boss is thinking about what this means to her personally. Chances are, she's going to be concerned and supportive—but you can also take this opportunity to show your concern and support for *her* job. You can tell her: "I know this leaves XYZ on your plate, but I'm going to do a full download to the team via phone so they know what the next steps are."

The same advice goes if you deliver much earlier than planned.

As soon as you're able, send an email to your office letting them know that you delivered the baby early. While you should punt on anything you're not ready to address yet, like how it will change the time you've planned for maternity leave, do try to give them a sense of when they'll hear from you again. (For example, "The doctor thinks we'll know more in a week, so I'll be in touch then.") When you're ready, do a short call with your colleagues to tie up any loose ends from your early departure, and communicate how you'll want to take your leave.

Email Auto-Replies

Given that we live in a day and age when most highly ambitious people are expected to be available by email from early morning until late at night, it's no simple feat to communicate "I am dedicated to my company" in tandem with "I have established boundaries." But that's a message you literally have to craft—your out-of-office auto-reply, and it is something many women agonize over.

Here are some ways you can frame your maternity leave out-of-office, as suggested by women who navigated their time away successfully.

SAY IT STRAIGHT

This is the plain and direct "I will be out of the office on maternity leave until _____" message, with a redirect to contact whoever is handling matters in your absence. This type of message is the norm in big corporations with infrastructure in place to fill any gaps. The biggest benefit of this approach is that you've set clear expectations about how responsive you'll be (not at all!), signaling you're truly unplugging, albeit temporarily—even if you surreptitiously check email now and then.

DON'T MENTION IT AT ALL

Omitting the word "maternity," instead saying, "I will be on leave until _____," establishes a different kind of boundary: one around your personal life and your privacy. This phrasing puts you on even footing with anyone else who takes time away, for any reason, removing motherhood from the equation entirely. A journalist told me she didn't specify *maternity leave* because she knew her peers were putting in long hours, and she felt guilty, as though taking time to be with a new baby was indulgent. But note: being this vague has its drawbacks too, as people may read too deeply into your leave, or misunderstand your absence.

MAKE IT PERSONAL

On the other end of the spectrum, you can use your out-of-office to update your colleagues and external contacts about your family. This is a great choice if you have a close relationship with clients and customers, especially if your professional success depends on those people feeling a strong personal connection to you. Caroline Logue, an account executive at Google, told me she included a link to her G+ profile in her footer: "Click here for updates and photos of Baby Logue!"

PUT THE BALL BACK IN THEIR COURT

One entrepreneur I spoke with set up an out-of-office that said, "I'll be offline until [date]. Please reach out to me after that date if this is not an urgent message." It's not the type of message you can use if you're in client services, but if your in-box frequently fills with emails from people you don't work with (like a reporter who receives story pitches), a blanket reply can allow you to declare "inbox bankruptcy" when you return. Instead of sifting through hundreds of messages from people you don't know well (or don't know at all), you trust that they'll follow up with *you* if it's important.

KEEP THINGS FLEXIBLE

In my own messaging it worked well to keep it intentionally vague about when I'd be available again. Though I still checked my email a few times a day, and I responded to anything urgent (like an email from an investor or a major partner) within twenty-four hours, this approach freed me to ignore anything that wasn't mission-critical. Conveying flexibility in your message with language like "Though I am checking emails, I may be delayed in responding during this time," can also help you accrue some working hours during your leave, which may enable you to extend your leave a bit or take an occasional Friday off to be with your new baby.

OTHER PRACTICAL MATTERS

Before your actual departure, you'll want to sit down again with HR to outline all your leave logistics and fill out any required paperwork. Here's a refresher on questions to ask, especially if you didn't get these answers in an earlier meeting:

- What forms do I need to fill out and when? (FMLA forms usually need to be completed thirty days in advance of your first day of leave.)
- How will I receive my paycheck? If I'm eligible for commissions or bonuses, how will those be paid out in my absence?
- How do I add my new baby to my health insurance?
- How do I sign up for a Flexible Spending Account for childcare?
- How do I add my baby as a beneficiary on my retirement or life insurance policy?
- When I return, where will I be able to pump? (If the accommodations are unsatisfactory, addressing this now gives HR time to remedy them. You're entitled to a clean, private space that isn't a bathroom; see more on this in Chapter 7: Returning to Work.)
- What happens if the baby or I have complications and I need to extend my leave?

Again, try to get as much as you can in writing from HR, even just by sending an email saying, "I'm writing to confirm what we discussed today regarding my leave . . ." Include every specific detail you can; if your company's handbook is vague (as most are), this is the closest you'll come to an official and comprehensive policy. (For a complete checklist you can download and print, visit herestheplanbook.com.)

Clearly, the key to a smooth maternity leave is developing a thorough coverage plan for your absence—which will benefit your manager and colleagues as much as it will benefit you.

WORTH REMEMBERING

- Take childcare transition time into consideration when you set your return-to-work date, and see if your employer allows flexibility for gradually ramping back up to full capacity.
- Put your coverage plan in writing. It's not just a practical way to help whoever is covering you; it also protects your professional turf and will help you in your transition back to work.
- Make sure everyone understands the protocol for reaching you—both how and when (once a week, just in an emergency, never, etc.). Consider designating an in-office gatekeeper who can serve as a filter.
- HR may have a ton of paperwork for you. Be sure to complete all their necessary forms (including but not limited to FMLA), and run through the checklist of questions in the "Other Practical Matters" section above.
- Schedule a meeting *now* with your supervisor for two weeks out from your return date. There's more in Chapter 5: Maternity Leave on what to cover in that conversation.
- If you'll be pumping when you return to work, take time now to block out half an hour every morning, midday, and afternoon in your calendar (say, 10:00 AM, 12:30 PM, and 3:00 PM). That way, you'll be less likely to return to the office with a back-to-back slate of meetings on your schedule.

CHAPTER 3

MAKING A CHANGE:
WHEN FAMILY PLANNING AND
JOB SEARCHING COINCIDE

K eeping your career on track during pregnancy is hard enough when you're in a stable, established job, but things get infinitely more complicated if you find yourself facing a job change (or career change) while you're starting a family—whether you're just thinking about getting pregnant, are already expecting, or have recently had a baby. You're simultaneously facing two daunting challenges: finding the right professional role (and selling yourself as the right fit for that role) and bringing another human being into the world. This chapter covers everything you'll need to consider if you're embarking on a job search while in the midst of growing your family: from when to disclose your pregnancy in an interview to how to assess whether a company *truly* has a family-friendly culture.

A former Navy officer told me she left military life because she didn't see any models around her of women with families. Not only was it logistically hard to fathom how to make her life work, she was also stuck in a culture where men repeatedly made references to their wives taking care of this or that for them. "What was I going to do?" she posed. "Go find a wife?"

She transitioned to the private sector, leveraging her years of experience managing a ship's nuclear reactor, and landed a job in a private power plant. She settled in, put down roots in a company that would provide a stable lifestyle, started trying to get pregnant, and then learned the whole plant was shutting down.

Seven days later, she got a positive pregnancy test. "I was panicked. I thought to myself, 'I have to interview before I'm showing!'" Fortunately, highly qualified nuclear engineers are in short supply, and she quickly was hired into a government agency. She didn't mention her pregnancy at any point during the hiring process. "I knew it wasn't supposed to be a factor in whether they offered me a job, but there's no way to know if it influences someone's thinking about you." When she showed up for her first day she was six months pregnant. Though she was ready to tell her boss, her orientation meeting with him wasn't until late afternoon. "I didn't take off my coat," she said. "I wore this enormous peacoat all day, telling people that I was cold because I'd just moved from California." She didn't want her boss to hear from anyone but her, so she laughed off comments like, "You must be sweating in that coat!"

When she sat down to meet with her boss, she was matter-of-fact: "I'm pregnant. I'm due in February." Her boss was nonplussed, and it didn't become an issue—and she feels like she lucked out.

Now, this is a somewhat unusual story, but it's not an uncommon situation, for a couple of reasons. The first is that, in many industries, you have to move around (either within your company or to another company) in order to move upward. There's nothing troubling about this—but it *is* still troublesome to calculate a move like that in the midst of planning for a family, either concretely (when you're already pregnant) or abstractly (when you're thinking about getting pregnant).

Layered on top of these complicated issues of upward mobility and timing is the second reason women find themselves negotiating a family planning/job search scenario: some career tracks and industries are simply inhospitable to working parents. Anything requiring extensive travel generally falls under this umbrella, as do jobs with unpredictable schedules or forced face time. Lindsay Cookson left her brand strategy consulting job not because she wanted or needed something that was "just" nine-to-five, but because she needed consistency and the ability to plan. She wanted "line of sight into the work."

By the time Jane Barratt had her third baby, she had achieved her career goal of running a Madison Avenue advertising agency. But those multiple maternity leaves had given her perspective. "You have a whole different reason to work," she said. "It's not just about jostling for position or money." She asked herself how she could create the sort of life she really wanted, and she realized that her ideal personal life wasn't compatible with her professional life at the time.

All of these women and many more I spoke with had to consider when and how to discuss their reproductive status in a job interview. Put that way, it sounds almost ridiculous that it would be a consideration, but I'm sorry to say that it is—and that's primarily because of unconscious bias. In the simplest terms, *unconscious bias* means you show favoritism toward people who feel familiar to you or you can identify with. The converse is also true: if someone feels too different from you, you're less likely to make her a job offer, extend a contract, or invest in her. Very smart, good, and generous people fall prey to unconscious bias, and, statistically speaking, you've most likely been on both the giving and receiving ends of it.

So, back to your reproductive status: everyone has a preconceived notion of what it's like to work with a pregnant woman or a new parent. And while sometimes that's positive (keep reading for a pretty rah-rah sisterhood story), more commonly it's not so positive. I realize I'm making some sweeping generalizations here, but there are a few standout "types" that can be especially hard on working mothers or soon-to-be working mothers:

MEN WHOSE WIVES STAY (OR STAYED) HOME WITH THEIR CHILDREN: In many cases, these fathers have been insulated from everyday hassles like picking up a sick child from daycare or getting home in time to relieve the nanny. Some can't imagine what life would be like in their household if both parents were working. "As enlightened as you may think the men in your office are," one woman explained, "there still can be a struggle if they don't have an example to look to in their own lives."

WOMEN WHO'VE BEEN THERE, DONE THAT: Don't assume you'll get automatic support or understanding from your maternity "predecessors," especially if they didn't have an empathetic boss or colleagues when they had a baby. There often is a "Do you know what *I* had to do?" mentality. "Tough love" can be a euphemism in these cases; the reality is tough toughness. They know how hard it is, but that doesn't necessarily mean they're going to make it any easier for you.

HARD-CHARGING YOUNG PROFESSIONALS WHO FEEL LIKE BABIES ARE IN THEIR *DISTANT* FUTURE: Katharine Zaleski, founder of PowerToFly, wrote an essay for *Fortune* about how judgmental she'd been of working mothers when she was in her twenties, describing how she'd assumed the mothers she worked with weren't committed to their careers. The article went viral, and she went on the *TODAY* show to talk about it. Now that she's experienced motherhood herself, she runs a startup that places working moms in jobs they can do remotely.

As I said, these are generalizations, and there are many, many exceptions to them. I note them because it's too easy to believe that everyone is open-minded. It's important to realize that there's a broad spectrum of discrimination out there—and that only the extreme end counts as illegal. (I discuss this more in Chapter 4: Family Responsibilities Discrimination and Pregnancy Discrimination.)

While many of the women I heard from found themselves changing jobs while pregnant, more often they felt "stuck" in a job specifically *because* they were pregnant. This might be because they'd finally accrued enough leave to afford six weeks off, or because they felt reluctant to give up that stability—especially if that stability came with great health benefits.

Both are valid reasons for staying in a job, and they should absolutely be part of your calculations about whether to stick around or look for something new. When I first started thinking about getting pregnant, I told myself I needed to be in a job for two years before I considered taking a maternity leave. But that was faulty math, as I hadn't taken into account that the clock would need to be reset if I wanted—or needed—to change jobs. Just as in the example above where the power plant shut down, you may not be in control of where you're working when you get pregnant.

But don't forget to consider the drawbacks of remaining where you are. If you're in the wrong job, it'll feel exponentially worse once you have to leave a new baby every morning for it. One woman told me, "If you don't like your job when you go out on maternity leave, you'll hate it when you come back." If you have to hold on there for financial reasons like paid leave, start thinking about your next steps well before your due date. Network, plant seeds—do everything you can to help you find something better to transition to after your baby is born.

"During my second maternity leave," one woman told me, "I leaned in in a big way." She could see she was getting squeezed out of her job, so she channeled her energy into searching for a new and better one. "I flew across the country for interviews twice before my baby was ten weeks old." Ironically, she enjoyed her maternity leave more because she was so busy. "I craved that structure," she said.

* * *

INTERVIEWING WHILE PREGNANT OR A NEW PARENT

"I held my head high, with my belly low."

—KATE HURT, SOCIAL SERVICES COORDINATOR FOR SOUTH CAROLINA

Whether you're going on a job interview, meeting a prospective client, or trying to get a startup off the ground, if you're a woman in your twenties or thirties, there's a fair chance the person on the other side of the table will be doing some math in his (or her) head about when you might have a baby. One highly successful entrepreneur shared how, when she went out to raise capital for her company, prospective investors asked her point-blank if she was planning on having a baby at any point in the future. Now, though questions like that can be a powerful trigger for some self-righteous indignation, in some ways it's better to have those sentiments out in the open. The problem really lies with the people who are wondering but *not* asking. You have no way to know whether your pregnancy, presumed future pregnancy, or new baby has any impact on the opinion others will have of you—and this is in part because they might not even be aware of it themselves.

When Should You Disclose Your Pregnancy?

All the women I spoke with who found themselves in the not-so-desirable position of looking for a job while adjusting to pregnancy or new parenthood agonized over how and when to bring up their family. So, when *do* you tell a prospective future employer that you're due with a baby? There are two camps here: the first believes you could potentially harm your long-term relationship if you're not up-front; the second is adamant that it's as relevant to your hire as would be a herniated disk for which you'll need surgery six months down the line.

DISCLOSING IN YOUR FIRST INTERVIEW

This is a gamble, plain and simple. You can take the rational, logical view on this and tell yourself you wouldn't want to work somewhere that didn't want to hire a pregnant woman, but rational thinking and logic don't always play into hiring decisions.

My perspective is that, when you're interviewing, you're (rightfully) expected to put forth the most compelling professional version of yourself: what you've achieved, what you bring to the table, and why you'll be an invaluable asset. By bringing your personal life into that conversation—and your pregnancy *is* your personal life—you're muddying the waters and introducing someone other than the professional rock star that you are. It's important to realize that even the most feminist, supportive, egalitarian people can be influenced by unconscious bias—and that this is not a flaw or a fault or a reason not to work for them. So, by focusing exclusively on your professional experience, you're helping them avoid that bias. As one woman told me, "I applied for a promotion within my existing company, and my supervisor said that, if I weren't pregnant, he'd have hired me in a minute."

All of that said, there are some instances in which you'll need to be completely open from the get-go. If you're joining a very small company or team—where there isn't a lot of infrastructure and even a short absence would have major reverberations—speak up early. Ruth Ann Harnisch, a philanthropist who runs her own foundation, said, "If a candidate fails to grasp, respect, and address the impact this condition will have on both of us, she will not be the ideal hire." By using the first interview—in part—to lay out your strategic coverage plan for your absence, you can showcase your initiative, critical thinking, and skill in communicating a sensitive situation. According to Harnisch, "It can be a *winning* strategy."

DISCLOSING WHEN YOU'VE BUILT
RAPPORT WITH THE HIRING MANAGER

One high-level executive had expected that when she got pregnant she'd start planning to transition out of her demanding, travel-heavy job. But she had no way to anticipate that there would be a major

TALKING ABOUT ADOPTION

For women who are in the process of adopting a baby, all time-lines go out the window—both for sharing the news of your pregnancy with colleagues and of disclosing to a potential employer.

One woman told me that when she interviewed with a major nonprofit, she shared up-front, "I don't have children now, but I am in the process of adopting." She knew she might have only a few weeks' notice that she'd been "selected" as an adoptive parent—and that notice could come in two weeks or two years.

She assured her new boss she would keep him informed. When a promising relationship unfolded with an expecting mother, she hesitantly let her team know by disclaiming, "As you know, I've gotten this far in the process before..." Then, as that mother's due date got closer, she started to put together her plan and shared it with them.

But not everyone is comfortable presenting that much vulnerability; you might recall that Fran Hauser in chapter 2 waited until an adoption was near-certain before telling her team, something she managed with just two weeks' lead time thanks to her extensive planning.

overhaul in her office—with nearly 100 percent staff turnover—which left her embarking on a job search when she was still in her first trimester. "I immediately felt like I was in a race to find a job before I was huge," she told me. "I didn't want to be interviewed as a mother; I wanted to be interviewed on my skills."

But the hiring process for the role she pursued was lengthy and involved: in addition to working through a headhunter, she had meetings with various other stakeholders and a number of formal, and informal, conversations with the man who would become her boss. "We'd meet for drinks, and I'd order a glass of wine that I barely touched." Since he was the one who'd be putting forth her candidacy to the chairman of the firm, she told him she was pregnant in their third meeting. (She wanted him to honestly be able to answer "yes" if he was later asked if he'd known she was pregnant.) But by then, fortunately, her qualifications had been clearly conveyed—so the conversations became more about the company wooing her than about her proving herself.

When she met with the head of HR, she was greeted with: "So, I've heard you're pregnant! Congratulations. We have a couple of women here who have kids." She paused, then continued with enthusiasm and sincerity. "One of them even has *two*!"

Of course, there's still no guarantee you won't be viewed as a mom first and prospective hire second. I know a new mother of twins who was laid off soon after returning from maternity leave; not surprisingly, she was cautious in her job hunt not to ask overtly about work-life balance. When she instead asked how their day was structured, she felt they looked at her askance. "They thought I was asking the mommy question."

Conversely, you might undermine yourself by making assumptions about your potential colleagues. A social psychologist who works in academia told me she panicked when she was hired at the same time as a woman who had been vocal about not wanting children. As an academic, she was evaluated and judged on how frequently she published, and she worried that the other woman would be far more productive than she could be. Without the constraints of children, her "competition" would be unhindered in her career. "But the funny thing is," she said, "I figured out quickly that she was *not* more driven. She does other things with her time. She goes kayaking!"

DISCLOSING AFTER YOU GET AN OFFER

Let's back up for a second and reframe the job interview process: what if interviewing was less about them choosing you, and more about you choosing *them*? Since we've been conditioned to think about wanting a job and working hard to get it, it can be difficult to make the mental

I am all for leaning in—and for not making career decisions based on your *future* interest in having children—but at some point you're going to have to face the present reality that your professional life is going to change. It's not going to be worse, or weaker, or whatever—but it will be *different*. And assessing how that new and different life will fit within your company's (or future company's) culture is critically important.

Luckily, there are websites that provide a great deal of useful information. Maybrooks (www.maybrooks.com) is building a comprehensive database of various companies' family leave policies, crowd-sourced from the input of real women who work in those companies. There you can find out how many weeks of paid leave are offered, other benefits like flex-time—even whether they have pumping space. Glassdoor (www.glassdoor.com) offers similar transparency, conglomerating employees' scores of many companies on various categories (like work-life balance) as well as reviews of their experiences working in particular positions. And Fairygodboss (www.fairygodboss.com) spotlights company reviews written for women, by women.

You can ask some direct questions after you receive an offer (I can't emphasize this enough: wait until you have the offer!), but there are some covert ways to dig in the meantime:

- When you're in the office, look for child-related artifacts: family photos on your potential boss's and colleagues' desks, kids' art, etc.
- Social media can be a gold mine of personal information. One woman told me she hunted down the Facebook pages of everyone on the team she was interviewing with to see if they had babies or kids in their profile photos.

- If you'll be working for (or with) a lot of men, try to figure out if their wives work. (You could try Googling the husbands to determine their wives' names—wedding announcements can turn this up, or captions in photographs—then looking up the wives on LinkedIn. Wedding announcements also sometimes include parents' occupations; seeing that your future boss has a high-powered mother is another great indicator that he "gets it.") And though it's not a hard-and-fast rule, I talked to a number of women who said there was a direct correlation between her working relationship with her boss and his wife's professional success.
- Track down someone who no longer works for the company. A warm connection is always best, but I know people who've gleaned valuable insights from cold-calling strangers. Think of it as a cultural reference check. (Don't worry about this research getting back to the company: you're being thorough, taking initiative, and demonstrating your genuine interest in the company.)

shift to thinking about yourself as the prize. Think back to your first experience with "real" job interviews (excluding internships or part-time jobs): you'd probably just graduated college, and you probably weren't bringing too much to the table. They were judging you on your potential. All you had to distinguish yourself was your GPA, some semi-interesting summer experiences, and your personality. At that point in your career, they were definitely choosing you.

But now you most likely have a lot to offer: experience, accomplishments, and relationships. And even if the job is a big step up on the career ladder, you will likely bring as much value to them as they're offering you. And you're going to need to take three months off in the next year. No. Big. Deal. That's the attitude you need to have when you start this conversation—whenever you decide to have it.

So, why is this pep talk part of the "after you get an offer" section? Because an employer typically waits until *after* making an offer to get specific about the terms of your employment, like salary and perks. Those terms are part of the offer, and it wouldn't be unheard of for a company to say something like, "We'd like to offer you the job, but we'll need you to move to Korea for three months."

Your side of this dance is the acceptance. They make an offer, and you accept—or not. And just as it's perfectly reasonable for them to introduce something unexpected at this stage, it's also perfectly reasonable for you to state that you'll need three months off in the next twelve months. In a perfect world, you'd already know about Korea and they'd already know about your pregnancy—but in a perfect world, there'd also be no unconscious bias or pregnancy discrimination.

Note that I'm not saying this is the right way to go; when and how to talk about your pregnancy is going to be very specific to your situation. But *do not feel guilty* about waiting to tell a prospective employer until you're certain that your pregnancy has not influenced their opinion of you. After all, the law is on their side here: until you've been at the company for twelve months, they have no obligation to hold your job for you—nor do they (at any point!) have any obligation to pay you while you're out. (This is a downer, I know.)

DISCLOSING ONCE YOU'VE STARTED YOUR JOB

Until I'd heard the pregnancy-hiding-peacoat story, I thought waiting until the first day to tell your employer you're pregnant was a terrible idea. And it still isn't the ideal choice, but there are extenuating circumstances in which you'd want to wait to share your news. If you've only been in email contact with your new boss since receiving the offer and want to talk face-to-face, you might want to wait until you're in the office. (In the peacoat story, the new employee and soon-to-be employer were on opposite sides of the country, and there were a couple of months of lag time between the offer and her start date.)

WHEN PREGNANCY IS A SELLING POINT

Giovanna Gray Lockhart was eight and a half months pregnant when *Glamour* editor-in-chief Cindi Leive hired her as their Washington, DC, contributing editor. When she started back at work after her leave, Lockhart remarked to Leive that she admired her willingness to take a leap of faith with her.

Cindi's response: "Oh, I do it all the time." She went on to explain that she understands that when you're pregnant, you're feeling especially vulnerable (professionally, emotionally, physically), so if someone is putting herself out there for a job in that time, it's a sign of ambition. "And those are the type of people I want on my team."

"I'd traipsed to New York in an ill-fitting dress to interview with her," Giovanna told me. She walked into Condé Nast feeling frumpy and not particularly hireable, and all she could think was, *She's going to notice I'm wearing flats.*

If Leive noticed, it had no bearing on her impression. She told her, "I really want you for this job." She didn't care that Lockhart was about to give birth; she explained that hiring her at 34 weeks was like an insurance policy. "If I wait until after you're ready to come back to work, you could decide to go somewhere else."

If you're accepting the offer when you're still in your first trimester, you can wait. You don't need to give an explanation of what you knew when, but if you feel you must offer a disclaimer when you eventually share the news, you can simply say, "It was too early to know for sure when we were talking about my joining the company," or, "We just found out that the pregnancy was healthy." Similarly, if you didn't know you were pregnant during the interview process or got pregnant before starting (as might be the case when interviewing during grad school), you might want to share the news in person.

Finding a Job with a New Baby

I talked with a woman who started interviewing for a new job when her twins were about six months, and she was asked point-blank, "Do you think you'll be able to handle an executive director position with infants at home?" She recognized that "question" for what it was: a presumption about her capacity as a working parent. "What was I going to say?" she posed to me, "'Oh yes! I forgot about those babies! I should *not* be pursuing this job!'"

Bias isn't tied to a big belly; it's rooted in people's often erroneous assumptions about how mothers behave—or *should* behave. Putting yourself out there as a new mother can be just as detrimental as putting yourself out there as a soon-to-be-mother.

But Kristen Stiles, a former consultant and founder of Sitter (www.sitter.me), disagrees with me. After her first baby was born, she realized the culture at her big consulting firm was diametrically opposed to the ideas she had about family and motherhood. Worse, she realized that she was her own biggest enemy when she was working there; she felt herself itching for her iPhone when she was with her baby, and she was perpetually running a to-do list in her head. "I had an epiphany that I couldn't go back to my job. I needed to make a clean break and reset my expectations for myself." She ultimately left because, in her words, "I didn't trust myself to say 'no' to things that would have been impossible." She needed to transition into a job that wasn't going to be as all-consuming, and she wanted to be very up-front with her new employer about her availability. "I was brutally honest because I didn't want to waste their time or mine. I wasn't going to pretend I didn't have a kid."

I started interviewing when my son was about six weeks old, and I censored myself with some of the employers I was considering. One in particular had a reputation for being a burn-out organization: there were horrible rumors floating around about how demanding the CEO was. I also interviewed with the COO, who'd just come back from maternity leave, if you could call it that: she took two weeks off and then immediately reengaged. Even though I was telling other employers, "I've just had a baby, and I need to fit my work into a nine-to-five schedule," I hedged with this organization because that kind of compartmentalizing seemed to go against the grain of their culture. I got an offer, and I turned it down—mostly because I couldn't imagine achieving anything akin to balance there.

If you're holding yourself back in an interview, ask yourself why. Good answers include: it's a private matter; it's irrelevant to the job; it could cloud their opinion of me. Bad answer: if I worked here, my family would have to come in second to my job.

I can tell you from experience that tackling a new baby and a new job in tandem is stressful and overwhelming, but that doesn't mean it isn't do-able. (It is!) And being aware of that is a good foundation for what's up next: how to handle discrimination.

WORTH REMEMBERING

- Think long and hard about when the right time is to talk about your pregnancy with a prospective employer.
- Similarly, reflect on how candid you want to be about having a new baby. There's no right answer; go with your gut.
- There are tons of great online resources that'll help you assess work-life balance at a particular company (like maybrooks.com, glassdoor.com, and fairygodboss.com, among others).
- Dig deeper with your own covert sleuthing to really understand the workplace culture at a prospective employer, but . . .
- Wait until after you've received a job offer to directly ask work-life-balance questions of your new colleagues or HR.

CHAPTER 4

FAMILY RESPONSIBILITIES DISCRIMINATION AND PREGNANCY DISCRIMINATION

W hen I first started working on this book, I thought "handling discrimination" would be a small subsection, an in-case-you-need-it inclusion for those, like me, whose experience was an anomaly. And then I started talking to other women.

An astonishing *one-third* of the women I surveyed or interviewed for this book reported they experienced some level of pregnancy discrimination or family responsibilities discrimination.[6] As to more nationwide figures: though much has been made of the fact that EEOC (Equal Employment Opportunity Commission) complaints have risen more than 30 percent in the past decade, the absolute numbers are still low, with only 3,541 complaints reported in 2013.[7] To do a back-of-the-envelope calculation on that: given that four million babies are born each year in the U.S., and more than 70 percent of those are to women who work, just 0.1 percent of women reported pregnancy discrimination in 2013. Yet my tally, through an anonymous survey, was twenty-five *thousand* times that.

So, why would so few women file claims of discrimination?

Well, first and foremost, protections for pregnant women in the U.S. are shoddy at best, with onerous legal requirements. Many courts require a plaintiff to identify a nonpregnant comparator, someone comparable to the person who was discriminated against who is not pregnant. In some instances, the required similarities are so extensive that it's impossible to find a comparator who meets the standards. "Very meritorious claims get tossed out of court," explained Cynthia Calvert, a management consultant and senior advisor at the Center for WorkLife Law.

Meanwhile, an employer can demonstrate equally poor treatment of a nonpregnant employee. ("We didn't allow Jeremy to work from home after his knee surgery. We don't discriminate.") In fact, in *Troupe v. May Department Stores*, the U.S. Court of Appeals for the Seventh Circuit actually used that language: "Employers can treat pregnant women as badly as they treat similarly affected but nonpregnant employees."

Another reason: women fear recrimination, not just in their current jobs but also in their long-term ability to advance their careers. They worry they'll be branded as a troublemaker or muckraker—with good reason. Back in 2011, my fiercely progressive attorney warned me: "Speaking up could be a career-killer."

One of the women I interviewed for this book was deep in the hiring process for a senior government job when she was pregnant with her first child. When she sat down with the cabinet-level official who was making the final decision on hiring, he said, "Well, if you think you can handle the demands of this job *and* a newborn . . ." and trailed off. It was demeaning, she told me, and it felt illegal. "But what am I going to do? File a complaint against a cabinet member?" Her career would have been over.

I heard about a young female startup CEO who was approached

by a big-name venture capitalist. "It's good that you're doing this now," he told the woman, "because once you have kids your brain will go to mush and you won't be any good at all!" This from a figure who could make or break both her company and her personal reputation should she choose to voice her objection to such comments.

And the last—and most common—reason for that huge discrepancy in reports of pregnancy discrimination: no one asked. Reluctant to pursue legal action (or even file a complaint with HR), most women feel there is nothing they can do or say.

As one woman put it, "I still don't think I had much middle ground. I could either take it on the chin, or scorch the earth. And that's because even a reasoned, thoughtful, level 'Hey, this isn't okay!' gets you labeled a liability."

Before you read any further, know this: there is a 180-day federal statute of limitations on discrimination cases (which has been expanded to 300 days in most states). That means, if you're laid off early in your pregnancy, by the time you're ready to head back to work you'll have exhausted that 180 days. So if you feel you're being mistreated, to keep all doors open talk to an attorney as soon as possible.

A BRIEF INTRODUCTION TO PREGNANCY AND CAREGIVER PROTECTIONS

The basic background: in 1978, Congress enacted the Pregnancy Discrimination Act, an amendment to Title VII of the Civil Rights Act. It prohibits employment discrimination "because of or on the basis of pregnancy, childbirth, or related medical conditions." In 2008, Congress went a (small) step further and amended the Americans with Disabilities Act to include impairments related to pregnancy, such as gestational diabetes or preeclampsia, and requires that employers make reasonable accommodations for those women. (Pregnancy is not a disability, but pregnancy-related conditions like preeclampsia or hyperemesis gravidarum can be.)

These protections are enforced by the EEOC, which also periodically publishes legal guidance that more clearly defines discrimination; they've extended their language to include "caregiver discrimination" or Family Responsibilities Discrimination (FRD), which often impacts women when they return to work post-pregnancy. In broad terms, FRD occurs when employers make assumptions about your ability or willingness to work because you have children—and that also extends to assumptions about future pregnancies or children.

City and state law can offer more protections: in Washington, DC, San Francisco, Philadelphia, and other cities, employers cannot discriminate based on family-caregiving obligations. That means that they cannot refuse to promote a woman because she is the mother of young children. In states without such laws, employees can bring FRD claims using sex discrimination and family-leave statutes. This is true even in states where employment is "at will."

All of that is to say: as a pregnant woman, you qualify as a protected class. But this *does not* mean your job is safe or that you're insulated from layoffs or from getting sidelined. Layoffs are particularly murky, because your position can be entirely eliminated. "I paid a lot of lawyers to tell me that it wasn't about me, but about the *position*," one woman told me. "It was the biggest rude awakening of my career. The role gets eliminated, and your company's hands are clear."

In one attorney's words, "There's a low threshold to file a lawsuit, but you need a preponderance of evidence to win it."

DISCRIMINATION IN LEGAL TERMS

Family Responsibilities Discrimination is the broad umbrella under which pregnancy discrimination and caregiver discrimination fall. The EEOC's guidance on caregiver discrimination gets specific on instances that qualify (or do not qualify) as unlawful discrimination, and the law is getting more and more expansive on what constitutes discrimination.

Most cases of discrimination are rooted in what's known as "maternal wall bias" or "pregnancy bias." For example, let's say a supervisor assumes that an employee who is pregnant or a new mother is no longer interested in doing her job or isn't capable of doing the work. As a result, the supervisor may start assigning rote work, taking away direct reports, or reducing opportunities for advancement. Or perhaps personnel decisions are made based on these assumptions: for instance, a training slot may go to an unmarried woman in lieu of a pregnant woman—as though there's a chance the pregnant woman may not return. This behavior is not necessarily hostile, but for many women, it registers as "off."

In broad terms, you can pursue a case based on a comparator being treated differently (usually a colleague, but in some cases *you* can be your own comparator), or you can pursue a case based on stereotyping (your employer takes action based on a stereotype, like the assumption that you're less committed to your job).

Most cases are filed under one of the following four banners.

Disparate Treatment or Disparate Impact

Disparate treatment means an employer treated a pregnant woman or mother differently from someone who is neither pregnant nor a mother. Such claims need to demonstrate tangible harm (an "adverse action" in legal parlance): a lower pay rate, reduced responsibilities, a missed promotion.

I interviewed one woman who was a star at her big multinational consulting firm. She'd been told that she was going to be promoted, both verbally and in writing, but about a month before the promotion was official, while out at a work dinner, a colleague teased her about not drinking with him. He asked point-blank if she was pregnant, and, put on the spot, she shared that she was. Champagne was ordered, she was toasted, and everything was A-OK.

When that year's promotions were announced, her name wasn't on the list. It knocked the wind out of her; she described it as one of those incredulous "Is this really happening?" moments. "It was the first time in my life I had to acknowledge being female," she told me.

"There were things along the way in my career that might have been deemed harassment, but nothing as shockingly female-specific."

Another woman went out on maternity leave in the final quarter of her company's fiscal year. When she returned, she received a bonus check that was *half* of what she'd received the previous two years. When she raised her objections to the partners in her firm she noted how, despite being offline for a few months, she'd led more deals than anyone else. She'd earned 100 percent of her bonus—not 75 percent and *definitely* not 50 percent. "Let's not look at the math," she'd said to them, "even though the math is broken. I was part of every major achievement we had this year, and I deserve to be compensated."

The challenge with a disparate treatment or disparate impact case is that it requires proof that the employer took action against the employee based on the employee's sex or pregnancy, and that usually necessitates a comparator.

Hostile Work Environment

While the classic instance of hostile work environment—for women, at least—is unwanted amorous advances, claims can also be brought based on protected categories such as gender (think "dumb blondes") and pregnancy. For such cases to prevail the treatment must be so pervasive and extreme that it interferes with work performance. The examples cited by the EEOC include commentary about how one's career is over because of pregnancy or assessments of weight or appearance. One case involved a woman whose boss, soon after she announced her pregnancy, told her he was going to call her "prego"—and then did just that in most of their interactions. Soon after, he suggested she quit or go out on disability if she couldn't handle the stress of pregnancy.

One tech CEO I talked to ran up against a clueless and misogynistic board. One of her investors told the others, "I went crazy with hormones in my last months of pregnancy, so I have reservations about [the CEO] leading the company during that time." Unfortunately, while that may *feel* like a hostile work environment, a statement like that wouldn't meet the legal standards of pervasive and extreme unless she could demonstrate that it interfered with her ability to do her job—a difficult task, to say the least.

Failure to Make Accommodations

Because the update to the Americans with Disabilities Act took effect in 2009, we're really just starting to see accommodations cases make their way through the courts. Employers are required to make reasonable accommodations for employees who have physical impairments that limit a major life activity. This can include conditions associated with an employee's pregnancy, like carpal tunnel syndrome or gestational diabetes.

And since this is such new territory, there are still a lot of misunderstandings about what constitutes a disability. Employers are still learning about the requirements, and doctors are still learning about what they need to convey (and how they need to convey it) so employers will make the necessary accommodations. To address this, the Center for WorkLife Law established a working group bringing together physicians and attorneys, and they developed model statements doctors can make to employers (see pregnantatwork.org for more information).

Even if pregnant employees do not have a disability, they may be able to get accommodations from their employer using the Pregnancy Discrimination Act if the employer provides accommodations to other employees who have similar difficulties working. For example, if an employer provides light-duty assignments for employees who cannot lift heavy objects due to on-the-job injuries, the employer most likely will have to provide light-duty assignments for its pregnant employees who cannot lift heavy objects.

In addition, several states and cities have laws that require employers to provide accommodations to pregnant employees—even if they do not have a condition that rises to the level of a disability, and even if the employer does not accommodate other employees. These states include Alaska, California, Connecticut, Delaware, Illinois, Louisiana, Maryland, Minnesota, New Jersey, Rhode Island, Texas, and West Virginia.

Retaliation

Though it's difficult to prove discrimination, proving retaliation for making a complaint about discrimination is easy—in relative terms. There's usually a paper trail initiated by your initial complaint, and that initial complaint does not need to be deemed valid in order for you to be considered a victim of retaliation. It is enough if you can show that your employer took an adverse action against you because you complained that you were being discriminated against.

The EEOC's website has far more detailed guidance on what constitutes discrimination and what does not. In any case, an attorney is the best resource for assessing and understanding one's personal situation.

WHAT TO DO

If you feel you're experiencing discrimination, you have options. Here's where to start:

1. LOCATE YOUR EMPLOYMENT AGREEMENT, assuming you have one. Given that many employers require that you agree to go through a mediation or arbitration process before bringing a legal claim, that's information you'll want to have up-front.

Mediation and arbitration are both considered "alternate dispute resolutions" where a neutral third party facilitates a negotiation between the two parties. Arbitration can be binding, which means that the third-party individual comes to a judgment at the end of the proceedings, whereas mediation is not binding, meaning that both parties can walk away from the table if unsatisfied with the resolution.

2. Keep records of what's been troubling you. Keep a log of conversations or emails that trigger red flags, and hang on to any emails or documents that seem relevant to potential discrimination. For instance: if you used to be included in certain meetings, but now you're not; or you used to have your pick of projects, but now you're getting the dregs. Do your best to record your interpretation of such exchanges when they're fresh in your mind. Format these instances into a timeline, then incorporate your professional accomplishments (see item 3) and pregnancy milestones into it.

But a word of caution: this practice can be a little hairy because it can quickly devolve into what one attorney called "a paranoia diary." She explained that if you are pregnant and look hard enough, you'll find *something* objectionable, and "you could also go crazy keeping copious notes."

3. Build a dossier of your successes. Look specifically for measurable performance indicators that aren't impacted by bias (like sales figures). Be sure to consider people outside the company who can provide positive feedback (like client satisfaction surveys or customer compliments). If you don't already have feedback from them in your "praise" email folder, check in with them. Subtly fish for compliments: tell them that you loved working with them on XYZ, and you would appreciate any feedback they have for you. Also, get copies of your performance reviews; you may be able to use your pre-pregnant self as a comparator.

4. Talk to a professional who can give you an objective perspective. The obvious choice here is a lawyer, but a professional coach or even your doctor can also be a powerful resource. After two weeks of not getting calls returned by my office, I asked my OB/GYN if she'd had any other patients who'd had a similar experience. She suggested I start CC'ing her on my emails to my HR department, so she could be called on as an impartial observer.

A career coach can help you think through not just the next few months, but also what those choices and decisions might mean a few years from now. A coach can give you the employer's perspective, which is not always your rights-based perspective. Put simply, an attorney will tell you your rights; a coach will help you think about how to constructively frame a conversation with your employer about those rights. (Later in this chapter you'll find contact information for hotlines that help connect women with employment lawyers in their area.)

5. FIND OUT HOW OTHER EMPLOYEES HAVE BEEN TREATED BY YOUR COMPANY. Do your homework on the professional landscape within your company: do you have colleagues or peers who have been treated differently than you were? In many cases women with good discrimination claims lose because they can't point to a specific person who received different treatment.

It's important to have as many details about the other persons as possible: position, duties, length of employment, credentials, experience. You'll also need to explain in depth how they were treated differently in similar circumstances. For example, a woman with preeclampsia who was denied the ability to work from home might point to a colleague who was allowed to work remotely while recovering from appendicitis. A new mother who was laid off despite outstanding performance reviews might spotlight the single male peer with mediocre performance who was retained.

6. WORK WITHIN THE SYSTEM, TO THE EXTENT THAT YOU CAN. Cynthia Calvert, founder of Workforce 21C and a senior advisor to the Center for WorkLife Law, recommends initiating a conversation with your supervisor without making any accusations. If you've noticed you're getting fewer assignments, proactively express your interest in doing more. Your well-meaning supervisor may tell you that she avoided putting you on projects that required travel; Cynthia explained this as "benevolent discrimination."

Take this opportunity to express that, while you appreciate her concern, you care deeply about your role and want to ensure you have the breadth of experience you need to advance your career. Proactively affirm your commitment to your job. If the conversation isn't constructive or productive, your next step will be a meeting with Human Resources. But note: you may want to consult with an attorney first, because HR may try to secure an official statement from you.

7. DON'T SIGN ANYTHING! Even a seemingly innocuous document can include provisions that could be deeply damaging or unreasonably restrictive. When I resigned, my employer sent me a termination agreement that would have barred me from ever talking about any aspect of my professional experience there. (If I'd signed it, this book wouldn't exist.) Have a lawyer review any documents that require your signature. There will typically be a litigation clause that bars you from taking any further legal action; one woman lamented that she hadn't secured an exception allowing her to testify if called upon for a class action lawsuit (something she now includes in all of her employment contracts).

FINDING AN EMPLOYMENT LAWYER

Finding an employment lawyer can be more complicated than it sounds, because there's a limited subset of attorneys who represent plaintiffs in cases of employment discrimination. Most of the name-brand law firms that you know have deep, lucrative relationships with major corporations; these law firms represent them in tax matters, mergers and acquisitions, and contract law. It's bad business for them to take on a case against a company that currently is—or could at some point in the future be—a major source of revenue for them.

Case in point: I worked for the New York state attorney general for many years, so I know a *lot* of lawyers. And yet, when I found myself pushed aside in my job halfway through my pregnancy, I struggled to find good legal advice. From my outpost on the couch, I cast about vaguely, asking any lawyer I knew (including my high school boyfriend, who primarily represents franchisees of donut shops) what I could or should do. It was the equivalent of asking a dermatologist about how to treat migraines, but I didn't know where else to look. When I Googled "employment lawyer NYC," I found shady characters with big, blinking CALL NOW buttons emblazoned on their websites. They looked like the employment law equivalent of ambulance chasers—and definitely not whom I would want representing me to the Swiss investment bank I worked for. Ultimately, when push came to shove and I was looking at arbitration, I found someone through a family friend, but that was more than six months after the whole ordeal started. If I'd had a good attorney to advise me early on, I might have seen an entirely different outcome.

Initiating conversations with a lawyer does not mean you're escalating the conflict; you can get advice from a lawyer without your employer ever knowing you've retained someone. I know it can feel scary to acknowledge (even just to yourself!) that you may want to consider legal action, but getting a professional opinion early on can help insulate both your reputation and your paycheck.

And even if you ultimately decide to leave your employment because of your treatment during pregnancy, a good employment lawyer can help you negotiate a fair package. Your employer will ask for a separation and release agreement, in which you indemnify them and agree to a nondisclosure, and there needs to be some consideration for that. In addition to the obvious questions like severance and continuation of benefits, think about what will help you keep your career on track—and ask for *more* than you think you "deserve," such as outplacement services and a good reference. I know several women who negotiated the white-collar equivalent of "no-show jobs" so they could look for their next opportunity while still being technically employed.

Just be mindful: if you *do* bring a lawyer to the table, it will usually trigger some compliance procedures that can slow down the speed at which to find resolution.

Where to Look

A personal recommendation from someone you trust should always be your starting point, but most people don't even *know* that they know someone who has worked with an employment lawyer. (It's not exactly the type of thing you broadcast to social media, and most cases have a nondisclosure that prevents employees from speaking about their situation.)

The National Employment Lawyers Association (NELA) and the American Bar Association (ABA) can be good starting points. NELA has local chapters in many cities, and the ABA has standing committees on employment law. Both organizations keep their member directories behind a password, but you can go the old-fashioned route and pick up the phone to ask for a recommendation. You can usually find the names of the committee chairs or attorneys who are especially active locally; reach out to them directly.

The Center for WorkLife Law has a very thorough website (worklifelaw.org) as well as a Family Responsibilities Discrimination hotline. When they field your call, they'll ask you a series of questions about your situation and direct you to a local attorney who specializes in Family Responsibilities Discrimination. (A local attorney is important because you want someone with a deep understanding of your city's and state's laws; they're often more generous to plaintiffs.) The Center for WorkLife Law also has a database of more than four thousand cases, so they have an overarching sense of how different large employers treat discrimination claims. Some, for instance, will never settle; that's valuable information to have when you're gauging how and if you want to proceed with a case. A Better Balance (abetterbalance.org) and the Equal Rights Advocates Hotline (equalrights.org) offer similar services. (You can find links and contact phone numbers at herestheplanbook.com.)

One of the best pieces of advice I heard was to try to talk to three attorneys to get their individual, independent opinions on whether you have a case. Just as you wouldn't make a major medical decision without a second opinion, you shouldn't make a major professional decision without doing the same due diligence. A lawyer's interest in your case is going to hinge on whether he or she assesses potential recoverable damage. But, given that without recoverable damages there's no real financial incentive to pursue legal action, this assessment can be subjective.

Be aware, though, that many plaintiffs' lawyers do not offer free consultations; they simply can't afford to. As one attorney put it, "You get calls every day, and a lot of the calls are from people who don't have a claim." Since the average person doesn't have the financial resources to pay a lawyer's hourly fee for litigation, employment attorneys often take a contingency (a portion of the damages awarded), and so they have to feel pretty confident of your case's merits to take on a risk like that.

Here are a few questions to ask an attorney you'd like to speak with further:

- Are there fees involved with an initial consultation?
- Should we decide to work together, how are your legal fees paid? If there is a recovery of attorney's fees, will you still take your percentage [*usually 30 to 45 percent*] of my settlement?
- How will expenses, like deposition fees, be billed? Will I be responsible for them as they accrue?
- Can you tell me about any cases you've had that were similar to mine? [*You want to make sure that your lawyer has experience with pregnancy claims; or, if your case is related to the FMLA, make sure the attorney has filed FMLA claims.*]
- What do you think my recoverable damages may be?

You'll also want to assess your comfort and fit with the attorney. One woman explained, "This isn't like finding someone to represent you when you're closing on a mortgage." It's not just how affable you find the person, but also whether you feel empathy and understanding.

Some firms operate as litigation mills and benefit from doing tons of meetings; you'll want to ensure that the attorney is really *listening* to you. Consider too whether his or her presence is empowering and reassuring; if you enter negotiations or go to trial, you're going to want someone sitting beside you who not only *is* confident but makes *you* feel confident.

WHAT'S YOUR END GAME?

When you see newsworthy stories about extraordinary financial settlements (Millions of dollars! Tens of millions of dollars!), it's easy to start to see that kind of restitution as the norm. A recent case against AutoZone made headlines when a jury awarded a woman $185 million in punitive damages—an amount that's widely expected to be overturned. Those cases are newsworthy, though, *because* they're unusual—and they've also been tried by a jury. You don't hear about the private settlements, because they're covered by a strict NDA—and those settlements can be as low as a few thousand dollars.

There's no simple math to help you determine what your case might be worth, but, broken down, there are two components of an award: restitution and compensatory damages.

RESTITUTION is your employer making you whole for the amount of money you lost as a result of the unfair treatment you experienced. This is where the equation is a little simpler: your weekly wage times the number of weeks you were out of work as a result of your employer's discrimination. Of course, if you've been discriminated against as an *applicant*, you may have no restitution.

COMPENSATORY DAMAGES include emotional distress and out-of-pocket costs or other economic damages. You may also seek punitive damages, which may be awarded if your employer acted truly egregiously. There are federal statutory limits on compensatory and punitive damages, which are based on the size of your employer and range from $50,000 to $300,000. (If your employer has fewer than fifteen employees, you cannot sue under federal law.) Some states, however, have laws that apply to smaller employers and that provide uncapped damages, which is again why it's important to work with an attorney who is deeply familiar with the local law.

Note that the amount you're awarded for back pay and some other types of damages is taxed as ordinary income, and your attorney may still deduct a fee. And, again, it's all still a gamble.

For many women, the emotional cost is the real barrier (or driver). In my case, I'd been carrying around resentment and anger for months, and I didn't see an end to it unless I stood up and made my voice heard. I knew there was a chance I would be out a few thousand dollars in legal fees if I didn't have a favorable outcome, but I saw that as the price of my sanity and ability to move on. There was also a small part of me that felt good about doing the "right" thing; I derived some satisfaction from that, despite its cost.

While one nine-year veteran of a major financial services company was on maternity leave, two new organizational charts were distributed at her office. She wasn't on them. "When I got back," she told me, "I was managing two people. I'd been managing nineteen before I left, and I'd been promised a promotion." She told HR that they needed to give her the job she'd been promised or give her a buyout package. Then she consulted a lawyer, who explained that the only way she could get any compensation or prove discrimination was if she was willing to show up every day and be a thorn in their side. "It was so emotionally unhealthy. I was crying on the subway on my way to the office every morning." So she walked away.

Litigation is doubly costly in that you're looking at significant legal fees on top of a tremendous emotional expense. "Litigation is gut-wrenching," an attorney told me. If your claim includes an allegation of emotional distress, your employer's lawyers will have access to your health and mental health records. They will be very intentional and strategic in making you as uncomfortable as possible, because they want you to fold under that pressure. "If you've stated that the loss of your job strained your marriage," the attorney explained, "they could ask specific questions about your sex life." You may find yourself sitting in depositions, listening to your coworkers lie—and you won't be able to do anything about it.

But even if you decide not to move forward with a claim, you can still speak up. (But be mindful about using social media or a blog as an outlet for your frustration: before posting, think through the lens of a future employer stumbling upon what you've shared.) For one, you can talk to a journalist "on background," which means they won't use your name. Journalists need to talk to real people for stories they're writing about workplace equality and discrimination against parents. They often call sources like the Center for WorkLife Law; when you speak to someone at their hotline, you can tell them that you're willing to be interviewed. You can also testify to your state legislature when they're considering a bill to protect women's workplace rights—or better yet, contact your state representatives and ask them to introduce legislation to protect working women. (Though this should go without saying, ensure you're being completely truthful anytime you're speaking about an employer, and check beforehand to be certain you don't have any nondisclosure provisions.)

I hope you're not discouraged by this chapter, though I know it is a downer to learn this stuff (it was for me!). Moreover, I hope you'll never have to revisit it. The good news: should you encounter discrimination, you'll already know a lot more than I did when I was pregnant.

WORTH REMEMBERING

- Pregnancy discrimination is not always malicious, but it is incredibly pervasive.
- Log anything that feels like a red flag to you; keep documents, emails, and notes about conversations (so long as you do not violate your company's document policies).

- There's usually a 180-day or 300-day statute of limitations on employment discrimination; don't wait to call a lawyer.

- NELA (the National Employment Lawyers Association) and the ABA (American Bar Association, and its local chapters) can help you identify an attorney, or you can call the Center for WorkLife Law's hotline.

- Engage a coach to help you think through the long-term career implications of any decisions you're making; a lawyer focuses on just your rights, not necessarily on what is best for you professionally.

PART 2.
AFTER BABY ARRIVES

CHAPTER 5

MATERNITY LEAVE

Y ou might be thinking, looking at the title of this chapter, *Why are we talking about maternity leave? I thought this book was about my professional life.* But your mindset and experiences during maternity leave can carry over to your return to work, and the mechanics and logistics of several months home with a baby are too often glossed over. Women who have recently returned to the office, when asked how maternity leave was, often say, "It was great!" Few volunteer that they were lonely, or out of their minds with sleep deprivation. Some will wax poetic about the wonders of motherhood even if a couple of hours earlier they were starving for some indication they weren't doing this whole motherhood thing wrong.

You may also hear, "It's great to be back!" from women who are grappling with a gut-wrenchingly painful separation from their baby. One woman described those early days as "soul-killing, burst-into-tears-in-public awful." When I asked women what one word they'd use to describe their maternity leave, the most common response was "Short." And nearly one-quarter of the women I heard from called themselves "not remotely ready" to return to work at the end of their leave.

We're conditioned to be positive, especially when it comes to our children. And that's okay. But that relentless positivity can paint an unrealistic picture of what life as a new parent really looks like.

Put simply, maternity leave is *hard* for many women. After a few weeks, taking care of the baby usually starts to feel manageable. Your confidence builds in basics like changing diapers. Eventually, breast-feeding starts to feel a little more natural—or at least, a little less unnatural. (Unless it doesn't, which is okay too. More on that later.) *Self*-care is often where the wheels come off the bus, and I'm not just talking about finding time to take a shower or brush your teeth. I'm talking about doing things like feeding your brain, spending time with humans who can talk back to you, and doing things that are just for you—as you've been doing for the past couple of decades without even thinking about them. Those things get displaced by a baby, and they can disappear entirely if you don't work consciously at preserving them.

Then, just when you're starting to feel like you're getting the hang of this whole baby thing, and maybe even starting to figure out the "taking care of you" thing, it's time to go back to work—and that can feel different for everyone. Some women are itching to get back to the office, while others are devastated to leave their tiny babies. Many women feel both simultaneously, which makes sense: no matter how eager you are to get back to "real" life, it is incredibly hard to turn over a newborn to someone else for forty-plus hours a week. You may wish you had a couple of more weeks, or months, or even years at home with your new baby, and if that decision isn't in your hands, you might feel resentful or angry—or just plain *sad*.

One of the least fair realities of life as a working parent is that your baby is only a baby for a really short span of time. In obvious terms, that means that your window to appreciate and luxuriate in that babyhood can feel small. But it also means that this is the only time your baby is going to need you *this* much, all day long. You're only five years away from your kid having her own "day job": going to school every day for seven or eight hours. I talked to a lot of women who found it helpful to remind themselves of that—they were continuing to invest in their careers now, so they'd have fulfilling work later.

MATERNITY LEAVE OUTSIDE THE U.S.

We've already covered—in depth—how crappy the American system of maternal support is, from the limited time allowed for leave to the inadequate pay afforded to women recovering from childbirth. One Brit who had her babies in New York said, only partially in jest, "It's cruel and unusual punishment and a violation of human rights."

Other cultures approach postpartum mothers radically differently, with philosophies derived from a core recognition that having a baby isn't something you simply bounce back from: it requires time and support for both physical and emotional healing. It's important for us in the States to consider this broader context in defense against all the "shoulds" of new motherhood: "I should have my baby on a schedule already. I should be able to start working again once my baby is six weeks old. I should fit in my pants." In truth, "shoulds" are at best minimally helpful, and at worst paralyzing and agonizing.

When both of our daughters were about six weeks old, I met with a Chinese American first-time mother who is the U.S. CEO of an Israeli-based startup. Needless to say, she's a go-getter. During our conversation over coffee I asked what she'd been doing on her maternity leave and whether she was in touch with the office. I was stunned to hear this was one of her first outings. "I stayed home for thirty days. It's a Chinese tradition." She was talking about *zuo yuezi*, a series of restrictions for new mothers in the monthlong period after childbirth, including not leaving the house or taking a shower. (There are also onerous dietary rules, as well as guidance on how to dress and how much to cuddle the baby.) It's an ancient tradition with some modern updates, most notably a luxury postpartum hotel where mom and baby retreat for a month to be cared for by professionals. (These centers are popular among China's elite, but there's been an uptick in major cities like New York and Los Angeles.)

In Latin American cultures, that lying-in period is forty days and is called *cuarentena*. During this "quarantine" period the new mother's sole responsibilities are breast-feeding the baby and recovering her physical strength. To enable this, other female relatives step in to handle all household tasks, including caring for any other children.

For new mothers in the U.K., a midwife checks in on baby and mom for the first ten days home from the hospital. The midwife provides on-the-job training in newborn care, including how to give a bath and helping with breast-feeding support. France offers a similar program. As for length of leave: our northern neighbors in Canada put other countries to shame, allowing one full year of paid maternity leave.

So though it's unlikely we'll see anything comparable in the U.S. in our lifetimes, it is worth remembering, when those "shoulds" creep up ("I should be able to get the laundry done!"), that our expectations of new mothers are unnecessarily onerous.

REALITY WITH A NEWBORN

Bliss! Bonding! Mountains of free time!

For people who've never had a baby, there's this broad conception of maternity leave as an open canvas that you can use to enrich your life. You're making a lifelong connection with your newborn while also getting a few months to "yourself" that you can use to learn a foreign language and go on adventures. One woman told me her colleague kept making references to her upcoming maternity leave as her sabbatical. While she was pregnant with her first baby, Katie Duffy, the CEO of Democracy Prep Public Schools, told everyone she was going to watch *90210* episodes all day; she joked about it so often that her team bought her the boxed set.

But here's the unfortunate truth: many of the women I spoke to said they were unhappy or unsatisfied during much of their maternity leave. They often felt adrift—and they didn't like it. Duffy explained,

"I've always worked, since I was sixteen." For her, maternity leave felt like a void, and this makes perfect sense. If your identity is tied up in your professional life, and suddenly your professional life is on hold, who are you? Another woman told me, "I had no idea what people did all day if they weren't working."

There's lots of time alone in your own head. There can be boredom or frustration that you're doing the same thing over and over again. One woman told me she knew she'd completely lost her bearing when she called her husband at the office to tell him about that day's mail. "We'd gotten some kind of credit card offer. I actually picked up the phone to ask his opinion about this piece of junk mail." She was that hungry for human contact and something to talk about that wasn't the baby. Another said, "There's this idea out there that you should 'cherish every moment.' It puts a lot of irrational pressure on you. It doesn't make you a horrible parent to wish that you had your old life back."

Morra Aarons-Mele, founder of Women Online, had her first baby during a snowy winter in Boston. "I had this image of maternity leave being cozy and snug and domestic goddess-y," she said, "but I don't know anyone who had that experience." She found herself watching the clock all day and wondering when her husband would be home. Another woman told me that she cried when her mother went back home after the baby's first four weeks. "I just didn't know how I was going to do it alone."

My friend Margo's husband took two weeks of paternity leave. On the morning he headed back to work, his first meeting was at Margo's favorite breakfast place. "When he left for that meeting," she told me, "I was just sitting in my rocking chair with greasy hair. I hadn't taken a shower, the baby had just spit up on me, and it was a hot summer day." She melted down in tears. In between sobs she said, "*I* want to go to work!" She saw their life in black and white: "I was starving, he was off to a breakfast. I was dirty, he was freshly showered." It felt terribly unfair, and she just wanted some semblance of her old life back.

After my son was born, I felt unmoored because I didn't have any kind of measure of my productivity. I needed to have something to *do*. I tried to shoehorn my baby into a schedule because I thought that would help give me a sense of accomplishment and structure. (With no set schedule, it's easy to obsess about just how to survive the day.) But when I didn't achieve military-level precision in our feeding times and naptimes, I felt like a failure.

A music teacher from Boston shared: "In the early days, it was just so damn hard, and in the later days, it was mind-numbingly monotonous." In hindsight, she wishes she had created more of a schedule for *herself* and been less concerned about the baby's schedule. "Join moms' groups and *go*—frequently. Go to the breast-feeding support classes, even if you aren't having trouble. Go to baby yoga even if you have to drive forty minutes to get there." And most of all: "Forgive yourself if you don't find maternity leave to be amazingly blissful."

FEELING A LITTLE LESS ALONE

Naama Bloom, founder of HelloFlo, hated her first maternity leave. Engaging with the new moms' groups didn't feel natural for her, particularly because so many of the moms weren't returning to work. "I felt like a transient part of the community," she said. Fortunately she had one like-minded friend with whom she got together regularly, and they jointly lamented the lack of mental stimulation. "Wouldn't it be great," they asked themselves, "if mom groups assigned articles from *The New Yorker*, and that's what you'd talk about when you got together, instead of sleep schedules?"

"Even when people were around, I felt lonely."
—A RESEARCH ASSOCIATE, JOHNS HOPKINS UNIVERSITY

The second time around, she knew to build in structure for herself. For one, she was looking for a new job, which meant she got out of the house—without the baby—on a regular basis. She also signed up for a facilitated moms' group that she found through a Google search, despite having rolled her eyes at it previously. Everyone in the group had both a toddler and a baby, so there she found a deep commonality and a true sense of community that she'd been lacking.

As Naama did, you can find such groups online: search for a local parenting listserv, or try Meetup (moms' groups are their biggest constituency). Classes like baby yoga are great mom-matchmaking spots. Several mothers said, "The only reason to go to classes before your child is three months old is to find friends."

A Google employee told me she loved an exercise class for new moms. "It was the greatest thing. It was my lifeline." She happily found herself surrounded by people who were all going through the same thing at the same time. Her maternity leave became about feeling strong and together. Others called new-mom groups their "saviors."

But be mindful of the type of friends you gravitate toward: if they're all taking very extended leaves from work, or not going back at all, you might feel like an interloper. One mom told me she felt pressure, albeit unintentional, not to return to work because she was surrounded by women who weren't—even though she was pretty certain that working was the best thing for her and her family. Another said she felt jealous of the stay-at-home moms in her daughter's music class.

One type A mother said it took almost her full maternity leave to settle in to the transformation of her day-to-day responsibilities. "Instead of having five thousand people calling me and needing things, I had one infant," she explained. "I didn't realize how much easier it was until it was too late to appreciate it."

Selena Hsu loved her maternity leave, and she credits time spent in yoga pre-pregnancy with her ability to "be in the moment" with her baby. "I got practice at being present and empty-minded and open-minded," she explained. "I could be alone in my body, but instead of alone in my head in a yoga class, I was alone with a baby." But even within that relative serenity she found she had to scale back her expectations of herself. While she was pregnant she'd polled friends about short day trips she could take with a baby; she read articles and blog posts about how you can strap your baby to you and go to museums and out to nice lunches. But her son had terrible reflux and wasn't gaining enough weight, so feeding him became a major stress—and something she could really only do at home. "I didn't go to *any* museums. I didn't go anywhere. If I made it three blocks to Central Park, that was a big outing."

By the end of the fourteen weeks she took for leave, she was eager to get back to her job at Yahoo. She and her husband had always had a ritual when they got home from work: they'd share their days, talking about what they'd done or whom they'd seen. But during her leave, after a day attending to an infant she felt she had nothing to offer. "I felt like I was getting dumber and smaller," she told me. "I wanted to get back to reading things, writing things, creating things—and having things happen to me."

MISSING THE GOLD STAR

I have always been someone who seeks out validation; I pride myself on my professional achievements, and I crave some measure of proof that I've done well. I call it "needing a gold star."

With a new baby, there's no positive reinforcement of what you're doing; no one expresses gratitude for your contributions or commends you for outstanding performance. The best you can usually hope for is a lack of negative reinforcement: a baby who isn't crying or fussing. It's jarring to not know whether you're succeeding, and it's all too easy to end up channeling that energy into assessing whether you're succeeding as a mother.

If you're breast-feeding, that assessment sometimes takes the form of trying to determine whether your baby is eating enough. "Perceived insufficient milk"—women fearing they aren't producing adequate milk to nourish their baby—is a common enough phenomenon that it has a name. Some women will get a special infant scale to weigh the baby before and after nursing so as to calculate how many ounces of milk were ingested. Others run timers and keep charts of how often and how long the baby nurses. (The good news here is that it's called "perceived" insufficient milk for a reason; it's just your perception, and usually a faulty one.)

> **"**I went from traveling all over the world and managing fifty people to celebrating changing my pants every day.**"**
> —MARISA RICCIARDI, MARKETING CONSULTANT
> AND CMO OF NYSE EURONEXT

If you find yourself digging for validation or some measure of success, "step back," one woman advised. Set some reasonable goals for yourself, like getting out once a day, even if it's just to have coffee or look at the sky. She opined that too many women set unreasonable goals, like having a schedule or fitting into your jeans. "You can't squeeze this new person into your existing standards," she said. Another told herself every day, "I'm going to shower before my husband leaves for work and put on real clothes"—and that was enough to make her feel a little more human.

"It takes a while to get down a rhythm," one woman shared. "I had to learn my baby. I had to learn how to be a mom."

GIVING YOURSELF A BREAK

When my son was about four weeks old, we had a brutally exhausting weekend: Logan was up every hour through the night, and I'd reached my breaking point from sleep deprivation. I'd been home alone with him all day, every day, during the week and I felt broken by the experience. I was so tired and so lonely, and I just felt incompetent.

It's not uncommon for women to hold themselves up to a yardstick and measure their success against that of someone else. It's irrational and unproductive, yet we do it because we hunger for a benchmark. In my case, I seized onto the idea of pioneer women. I told myself, "If pioneer women could figure out breast-feeding, I should be able to." I imagined a rickety covered wagon and women in threadbare calico dresses and thought of myself as a huge failure. Months later, when I finally confessed this to a friend, she replied dryly, "Pioneer babies *died.*"

I desperately needed to hear that, though I didn't realize it at the time. Yes, it's a biological imperative to procreate, but caring for a baby is hard and fraught and scary—for everyone. I saw asking for support, or hiring it, as a sign of weakness. I had to get to the very edge of the cliff before I was willing to get help: and that weekend, staring down into the void, I reached it. More mentally and physically exhausted than I had ever conceived possible, I told my husband, who was gone twelve-plus hours a day, that I didn't think I was going to make it through another weekday alone with the baby. I saw a friend's post on Facebook about someone looking for work as a nanny, and even though I was months away from going back to work, I scheduled a coffee with her for the next day.

Within a couple of minutes of sitting down with me, our prospective nanny, Liliana, asked if she could hold Logan. As she scooped him out of his stroller a beaming smile stretched across her face. She lit up. Looking at her across the table, I thought, *I need this woman in my life so I can feel like that when I hold my baby.* She looked radiant; I just felt depleted.

That one decision entirely changed the tenor of my leave: for five to ten hours a week, I got a break, which I used to go to networking meetings and job interviews. Sometimes I just used it to nap. This support doesn't have to come from a paid sitter: many of the women I spoke with relied on family and friends—though you have to feel empowered to ask them for help. So ask, or hire someone. Just having those few hours of alone time on the horizon can provide so much relief when you're in the worst of it.

HIRING HELPERS

There are growing fields of professionals ready to provide hands-on care in the early weeks after delivery, specifically baby nurses and postpartum doulas. They're seasoned experts who provide, in addition to simply another adult able to ease the burden on the new mom, guidance on specifics like bathing a baby or starting sleep training.

This level of support can be particularly helpful for ambitious moms who need to ramp back up to work more quickly. Note, though, that it's a very expensive option—a safe estimate would be to ballpark two to three times what you'd spend for a "regular" sitter per hour. And while some people aren't comfortable having someone they don't really know in their home during such a transitional period, others say, as one woman told me, "It was the best money I've ever spent in my life."

Alternatively, and usually far less expensively, you can ease the burden on yourself by taking chores like cooking and cleaning off your plate. Hire someone else to do anything you don't *have* to do yourself.

In this digital day and age, you can add services like these to your baby registry—so rather than inundating you with newborn onesies, your loved ones can contribute to a baby nurse fund or pay for a house-cleaning for you. (You can do this at www.weeSpring.com!)

The less exhausted and depleted you feel when you return to work, the easier that transition will be. It's not indulgence or laziness to hire help during your leave: it's an investment in your professional life.

MAKING CHILDCARE A FAMILY AFFAIR

In her April 2009 article in *The Atlantic,* "The Case Against Breast-Feeding," Hanna Rosin described the piling on of responsibilities that can naturally emerge from motherhood. She writes about breast-feeding mothers: "She alone fed the child, so she naturally knows better how to comfort the child, so she is the better judge to pick a school for the child and the better nurse when the child is sick, and so on." This is true of breast-feeding, but it also is true of *any* mother who takes leave for care for her new child while her spouse returns to work. She gets "better" at childcare and household tasks, simply because she's had more practice.

When Sheryl Sandberg's *Lean In* was published, "make your partner a real partner" became a mantra for me and for countless other women. Yet the reality remains that in many households women bear a disproportionate share of family responsibilities—and, societally, we don't spend much time talking about specific ways to divide household responsibilities equally. Without a clear model of how successful families manage their day-to-day lives, it's hard to establish a framework that will put that theoretical "we're partners!" mentality into practice.

Even with a feminist husband (or wife), you'll likely need to consciously work at bringing your spouse on board as an equal partner. Countless little responsibilities crop up when you have kids, like remembering to schedule medical appointments and prepping and packing food for daycare. Individually, these are small tasks, but collectively, they're burdensome. Be deliberate about who takes on responsibility: make a list and divide it 50/50. You don't have to cleave to these assignments, but they're a good framework for a balanced partnership. (There's a worksheet on herestheplanbook.com that you can use as a starting point.)

> **"**In my low moments that I'm not proud of, I wail 'I'm so glad you always ask what you can do but I don't want to have to be the one who always thinks of what needs to get done!'**"**
> —A MEDIA EXECUTIVE, NEW YORK CITY

One key consideration before you start divvying up your list: planning and organizing and just plain-old *thinking* about this stuff are serious work. When you have a kid, you don't just have to make pediatrician and dentist appointments, you also need to find recommendations and vet those health care providers in the first place. You don't just have more laundry, you also need to acquire those clothes, whether they're hand-me-downs or newly purchased. (And babies grow out of clothes *fast*! You're constantly in acquisition mode.) One woman explained, "I'm generally the one who thinks, *We need to start*

HOW FAMILIES DIVIDE AND CONQUER

Here are some ideas from parents who've invested time and energy into establishing an equal partnership:

BE DELIBERATE AND CLEAR ABOUT DIVIDING RESPONSIBILITIES. When Maryhope Howland Rutherford, an academic social psychologist, saw a pattern emerging in her household in which she was becoming the primary caregiver, she established a Google calendar outlining the baby's life. She and her husband plotted out the hours they had childcare coverage (like daycare hours and babysitters), and they divided the rest up 50/50, including the middle of the night. She insisted that they follow it to the letter until they'd internalized that they were both equally responsible for their baby. "It sounds so obvious," she said, "but you have to look after a baby twenty-four hours a day." Mapping out each of those twenty-four hours was her way of bringing her husband on board with this reality.

ALTERNATE BEING "ON" IN THE EVENINGS. When I was organizing an event for working mothers, someone told me, "Women with kids won't show up to something at 6:00 PM." She paused, then added, "But their husbands do." Avoid that trap by assigning days of the week to each parent for daycare pickup or relieving the nanny. One woman described it as "being the six o'clock parent": one parent does Mondays and Wednesdays, the other does Tuesdays and Thursdays—which means both can get in some networking or socializing two nights a week.

SPLIT UP MORNINGS AND EVENINGS. One psychologist told me that when she works with new parents she encourages both to take the Morningness-Eveningness Questionnaire (available online), which assesses—as the name suggests—whether you're a morning person or an evening person. "More often

→

than not," she said, "the two parents aren't the same chronotype." Knowing which they are can help them organize their time so they can both be more rested. Putting that theory into action, Professor Alexandra Roberts told me she and her husband split night duty right down the middle. "Our default rule is that anything until about 2:00 AM is my problem, and anything from then on is my husband's. He's a morning person and functional at 5:00 AM. I, however, am not."

OFFLOAD EVERYTHING BUT FEEDING THE BABY TO YOUR SIGNIFICANT OTHER. Because I was breast-feeding our daughter, my husband, Jack, was in charge of feeding our toddler, himself, and me. He also managed what I called "output" (changing poopy diapers), because I did all of the "input" (nursing the baby).

DIVIDE UP HIRING AND MANAGING CHILDCARE. When my son was born, I took responsibility for finding our nanny, paying her, and coordinating with her, and Jack took ownership of any other childcare we needed. If our nanny was out sick, he was responsible for finding someone to cover; he was also in charge of finding extra coverage if we both had early morning meetings or late nights in the office. He booked all of our date night and weekend sitters, too.

considering X very soon. What information do we need in order to make that decision? In exchange for me doing all this planning, my husband happily and enthusiastically does the tasks—and in fact does many more of the tasks than I do."

Being the sole planner can get pretty lonely. A director at the Stanford Graduate School of Business reports having "decision fatigue," in which she's cripplingly exhausted by having to make all of the choices. Planning is emotional and mental labor; remember that, and make sure your partner understands this too.

That said, it's not *just* about the father taking on responsibility—it's also about the mother relinquishing it. "I'd do more," one dad told me, "if she trusted me to do it right." One friend scheduled herself a night out every week starting when her daughter was three weeks old. "I got out of the house for two hours," she said, "and it gave my husband the chance to be alone with the baby and learn her rhythms, without me hovering over him."

NETWORKING WITH OTHER MOTHERS

We talked in chapter 2 about the importance of seizing the opportunity to network before you're constrained by your daycare's hours or nanny's schedule. But you can also network with other new moms during your leave and after. Because being a new parent can be so isolating, new parents often are more open to making totally new connections. "It's kind of like college orientation," filmmaker Lacey Schwartz told me. You're at this big moment of change, and you're eager to meet the people who'll be in the same boat as you for the next few years.

She asks her friends for introductions to people they know with babies of her own baby's age. Sometimes she finds herself unintentionally conducting business during playdates, when a casual "So, what do you do?" uncovers some interesting intersections and opportunities to collaborate. Schwartz also does what she calls Baby Happy Hour: a relaxed, late-afternoon Friday gathering where a group of parents get together, have a drink, and talk shop—and just happen to have their babies along with them. When she lived in New York City, they met on the roof deck of her building; now, they go to someone's home in New Jersey.

"You make a whole other level of connection," she explained, "because you're being who you are, completely and totally." Instead of getting coffee and making small talk, the way you might have in your early twenties, you're weaving your business life into authentic conversations about the day-to-day challenges of being a working parent while you each juggle a baby on your arm.

OTHER CHECKLIST ITEMS FOR DO-ERS

If you need something to *do* during your maternity leave, here are some ideas from the parents I interviewed:

SCREEN BABYSITTERS AND BUILD A BACKUP STABLE. A caregiver safety net is the key to your smooth transition back to work. The next chapter has more on the specifics of finding caregivers, but even if you have childcare locked down already, you'll want to have at least three backup sitters (though aim for six). Hire a new sitter for a few hours when you'll be at home so you can see how she interacts with your baby. Store the ones you like in your phone with "babysitter" as their last name or title, so you have a list at your fingertips when you need it.

PREPARE FOR FEEDING YOUR BABY WHEN YOU'RE NOT AROUND. If you're breast-feeding, start building up your milk store (there are tips for that at herestheplanbook.com). If you're looking for a sense of accomplishment, there's little to rival a neat stack of frozen breast milk bags in your freezer. As one woman put it, "The spare milk is your freedom." Without it, you can't leave your baby for more than a couple of hours. (Formula can also bring freedom, so don't panic if you haven't been able to pump enough to fill your freezer; more on that later.) You'll also want to start introducing your baby to a bottle.

FIND A WALKING BUDDY WHO ALSO HAS A NEW BABY. This isn't just about having fun or being social. It's prescriptive for several reasons: light exercise helps your body recover and stave off postpartum depression; you can talk to someone who gets what you're going through; and you add a little structure to otherwise too-open days. One woman I interviewed signed up for a marathon while pregnant; while that may be too extreme for most, she loved having the structure of a strict training schedule.

GET YOUR LEGAL AND FINANCIAL DUCKS IN A ROW. In the appendix, you'll find information about drafting a will, buying life insurance, and doing the other things necessary to ensure your child is provided for should the unthinkable happen. Get these documents together, and keep them in the same place as your baby's birth certificate and social security number once you have them.

"PRACTICE" GETTING OUT OF THE HOUSE. The more you get out, the easier it gets. Take advantage of these early days when you can socialize with a sleeping baby in a car seat on a restaurant floor, or wear your baby in a carrier out to brunch with your friends. Your baby won't be this easy to tote for very long.

DIVIDE AND CONQUER. Use your leave as planning time for how you and your spouse will divide up responsibility when you return to work. Use the ideas earlier in this chapter as a starting point, and have a road map in place for what your spouse will take on once you're back at the office.

FEAR OF MISSING OUT

Plenty of the women I spoke with were happy to occasionally (or even frequently) engage with their offices. Some had check-in calls scheduled; others just stayed in the loop via email. Others saw their colleagues socially, whether coworkers stopped by to meet the baby or the new mom and newborn went in for lunch with the team.

But a note of caution about the news you hear from work: try not to read too deeply into the nitty-gritty of what you're looped into. Worrying about what that email about the client being difficult *really* meant can land you in a rabbit hole of anxiety.

When my friend Jill was on her maternity leave, she received an email from her boss that said:

Can't wait to have you back! Hope you're enjoying your leave.
PS: You really have to come back. I actually worked a weekend.

While Jill knows this was written with the best of intentions, there's still a subtext indicating her leave was a burden to her colleagues. Now, you can do a lot before your leave to mitigate resentment from colleagues, or make sure that XYZ project is properly handled. You can also do a lot when you come back—but there's not much you can do in the few months that you're home. Do your best to go easy on yourself.

One woman warned that responding to emails and engaging in any way can open up a torrent of questions and requests. Depending on whom you've left in your stead, there can be a slippery slope that starts at "occasionally accessible" and ends with "required for every decision." A former Warner Bros. executive warned, "It's especially hard to draw a nuanced line in a big company because of the nature of the culture. If people think you're on email, you'll get a ton. If they think you're off, you won't."

Theodora Konetsovska was an investment banker at Goldman Sachs when she had her first child. She advised, "If you're feeling tempted to log into work because you're lacking intellectual stimulation, read a challenging book." Jenny Cookson, a PhD candidate and managing editor of an academic journal, concurred: "Feed your brain," she said. "You become helplessly task-oriented when you're home all day. Dive into something philosophical or something historical that helps you feel like you're learning."

All this being said, I asked everyone I talked to what they'd do differently with 20/20 hindsight, and only 1 percent said they wish they'd stayed more connected. (Of the others, 82 percent had no regrets, and 17 percent wished they'd unplugged more.) One astute mother noted, though, that checking email doesn't mean you have to *answer* email. "Checking in on my email weekly helped me cull the junk and not feel like I was light years behind when I came back, though I only answered one or two emails over the course of my leave."

Particularly if you feel a lot of professional or personal responsibility for your organization, you're likely to feel some nagging anxiety about what's going on without you. The CEO of a nonprofit told me that she trusted the people she'd left in charge, but she had a longer tenure at the organization than anyone else and had amassed an expanse of knowledge that no one could match. "No one else was looking through the lens I looked through," she said, and the calls she'd get from her team reinforced that assessment. Unfortunately, "they didn't loop me in on some really high-stakes issues," she confided, "but they *did* call me about stupid details."

She watched at a distance as the culture of her organization changed. "I had thought about responsibilities and work flow," she said, "but I hadn't anticipated how the personality of the people left in charge would become the personality of the organization." Worse, she worried that the vacuum she left would be filled by someone who was angling for her job.

One media executive's second child was born during a tumultuous time for the company. At the very beginning of her leave, a new CEO was announced, and her peers and colleagues started calling, telling her she needed to be there because the new CEO was forming relationships—and she was going to miss the boat. "A new CEO bonds with some people and doesn't bond with others," she said. "Any leadership change like that puts you in a vulnerable place."

She had been at the company for eight years with an outstanding track record, but it didn't feel like enough. Being out of the office with a new boss she'd never met shook her confidence. "My brain was thinking: *She'll make decisions about the senior team, and all she'll remember about me is that I was the woman out on maternity.*" Thinking it was all or nothing, she rushed back when her son was just five weeks old, and she still regrets it. She wishes she'd gone back part-time, or less. "I should have gone in, met with her for a nice lunch, gone home, and scheduled another couple meetings."

RECONNECTING WITH THE OFFICE

Reengaging with the office toward the tail end of your maternity leave can help ease your transition back. At the very least, you should check in with HR and your boss in your last two to four weeks of leave to lock down logistics. (The "Worth Remembering" list in chapter 2: Putting Your Plan into Action recommends scheduling an in-person meeting with your supervisor for two weeks before your return.)

This meeting is the time to confirm your exact return date. For this, some moms advised setting that day midweek, say on a Wednesday, so you have a weekend on the immediate horizon. And though you might think it goes without saying that you are definitely returning, since you're setting a return *date*, be sure to articulate your commitment to your career and your company. Specifically reference the work that you're most interested in reengaging with; if your boss will need to assign projects or clients to you, use this conversation to ask for that work.

Touching base with colleagues and direct reports can be formal or informal, online or in person. Fran Hauser, who stepped away entirely from her role as president of digital at Time Inc. for thirteen weeks, set up a series of back-to-back coffee meetings in the coffee shop downstairs from her office. She made them social calls, but also got a full download of what had happened in her absence from each of her eight direct reports. In addition to just broadly catching up and getting the big picture, she asked them about their P&Ls, major developments, upcoming opportunities, challenges, and bottlenecks on which they'd need her help when she returned. "It was so helpful to do," she said. "It would have been a major shock to my system to walk back in blindly."

The platitude "the days are long but the years are short" pretty much applies to your whole life as a parent, but never more so than during that early time home with a new baby. The days are long, but those months (or weeks, for many new moms) are all too short.

WORTH REMEMBERING

- Take care of yourself. (If you don't, no one will.)
- Finalize your childcare arrangements, including a backup stable of caregivers, and allow some time for trial runs.
- If you're breast-feeding, make sure you have at least a few days' worth of milk in your freezer.
- A few weeks out from the end of your leave, reconnect with your office. Talk to your boss about your reentry plan, and have some initial conversations with colleagues about what you've missed.
- Get your partner on board. If he or she has been back at work, your return to the office may be the first time he or she has to *really* participate equally. Hammer out all the details of who will be responsible for what.

CHAPTER 6

HIRING A CAREGIVER

L ynn Perkins, the founder of UrbanSitter, travels the country giving talks to groups of parents about how to find a great sitter or nanny. The first slide in her presentation reads EXPECT CHANGE. This simple yet powerful advice applies universally to every childcare situation. So many women return to work with their hopes pinned on a specific and narrow solution, and then when something goes awry it throws their entire life into chaos.

And I cannot emphasize this enough: having reliable, responsible childcare is the foundation of your professional success. If you're fretting throughout the day about whether your baby is getting the developmental support she needs, if you're chronically late for work because your babysitter is chronically late, if you're missing important meetings because your baby has a cold and can't go to daycare, *you will not be your best at work.* It sounds obvious, and it is, but even the most meticulous women often expect that Plan A is enough because they worked so hard to get that Plan A in place.

I had a nanny lined up six weeks before I was scheduled to return to work, and I loved her: she was hands-on, experienced, warm, and everything else I needed to feel comfortable leaving my new baby in her care all day. A couple of days before my first day at the office, though, she told me she was having trouble with her asthma—and she thought it might be our cats. As you might expect, I was a wreck: I called my mother, weeping, asking if she could drop everything and come stay with us so I could start my (brand-new) job on schedule. I started texting friends, asking if they knew anyone. I mentally composed emails to my new boss, trying to figure out how I could possibly postpone my start date.

In short, I was totally derailed. In the end, I bought our nanny some Zyrtec and that resolved the issue entirely, but it was a wake-up call that even the most stable and perfect arrangement can shift in an instant. "It's always going to be a work in progress," one woman said. "Just when you think everything is great, you'll have to change something."

That change can throw your or your spouse's professional life into complete disarray. When I interviewed Margaret Wheeler Johnson, the managing editor of *Bustle*, her nanny had just quit. Since Johnson's wife, a freelance art attorney and advisor, had the more flexible schedule, they decided she'd be the one to screen new candidates—though she still essentially had to put her practice on hold for two weeks. "She is not enjoying being suddenly thrust into being a stay-at-home mom," Margaret told me.

No matter what your childcare arrangements are, be proactive about maintaining a deep bench of backup helpers. I store all of mine in my phone with "babysitter" in the title field, as I suggested in the last chapter, so I have a ready and searchable list that doesn't require me to wrack my brain.

When you're a first-timer and hiring someone to care for your new baby, every decision feels terribly (and understandably) fraught. But as one pragmatic mother put it, "I personally didn't feel my daughter needed anything too complicated at such a young age—other than a safe place to play." She found a daycare that was convenient, clean, and where her daughter was happy and well tended. That was enough.

Just "enough" can be hard to stomach when you're looking at how crippling the costs can be. "I knew childcare was expensive," Tracy Rahal, a Boston attorney, told me. "I didn't know it was 'year of private college tuition with room and board' expensive." Her son spends three days a week in daycare and two with his grandparents, and even that, she said, "is 'year of in-state college tuition' expensive."

Regardless of the form of childcare you opt for, a dependent care Flexible Spending Account (FSA) can help offset the mind-blowing costs. Similar to a health care FSA, a dependent care FSA diverts up to $5,000 a year from your pre-tax paycheck into an account that can be used for any on-the-books childcare expenses. Note: this $5,000 is a per-family allowance, not per-parent. At the end of the year (or periodically throughout the year), you file a form and get reimbursed for those expenses. As with health insurance, there's a once-a-year open enrollment period for an FSA, but the birth of a child is considered one of the "life-changing events" that allow you to change your election. You have thirty days after the birth of your child to enroll, so be sure to ask your human resources department about getting set up with a dependent care FSA *before* you go out on maternity leave—and while you're at it, ask about any backup care programs they may offer to employees.

In the face of the staggering cost of childcare, many women told me they asked themselves whether it makes economic sense for them to work. But "Do I want to work?" is a very different question from "Is it worth paying for childcare?" If the answer to the former is "yes," then the answer to the latter is too. Childcare is an investment for your family in the long term; it's not just about how much money is being siphoned from your paycheck for three to five years.

I wish I could say there was a silver bullet or secret handshake that emerged about how to find the best care for your child, but there's no right answer—there's just what's right for you and your family. "Trust your gut" is a terrible cliché, and one that's far more philosophical than practical, but the notion of maternal instincts emerged for a reason. Go with yours. In one woman's words, "If something in your childcare situation feels fishy, it very well might be." Dig deeper, and if there is a problem, fix it right away.

Of the women I heard from in researching this book, many felt they were way more worried about childcare when they were pregnant than they needed to be. Indeed, 58 percent rated themselves somewhere on the "concerned"-to-"panicked" spectrum—yet only 6 percent were unhappy with their childcare after their babies were born. And 23 percent used the word "amazing!" to describe their childcare.

In this chapter you'll find an abridged review of the various childcare options. (Much more information is available at herestheplanbook.com, along with hands-on advice, like questions to ask a nanny or daycare and how to run a background check.) I talked to women with babies in daycare or Montessori, women who had full-time nannies, women who were part of a nanny share, and women who used an au pair. There are *many* pros and many cons to each, so I encourage you to keep an open mind about what situation will be best for you. (And while I know there are wonderful male caregivers out there, for the sake of simplicity I'm going to use the female pronoun universally for this section, as I found that at least 95 percent of caregivers are women.) I also cover stay-at-home dads and family care at the end of the chapter.

And when you're thinking about your schedule for starting back to work, be sure to build in some transition time. If you're going with daycare, you'll want some dry runs, where you drop off your child but are still available to return in case of a problem. If you'll have an in-home babysitter, you'll want to spend at least a couple of days both showing her your routines and building rapport.

FINDING TRUSTED RECOMMENDATIONS

Regardless of whether you're looking for a nanny, nanny share, daycare, or au pair agency, most people start with recommendations from their peers: friends in the neighborhood, professional colleagues, new moms whose advice you trust. Send an email out to every newish mom you know, post to your social media, and be on the lookout for others' posts. (I found our nanny because a friend mentioned her on Facebook.) But for many, new-parent email Listservs or Facebook groups can be an invaluable resource.

Most cities—and even neighborhoods—have these lists and groups, with some much more deeply established. (Park Slope Parents in Brooklyn, New York, has thousands and thousands of members; another group, Berkeley Parents Network in California, has built a huge and well-regarded community.) New parents are happy—even eager!—to offer their advice and support, so these lists and groups tend to be very active. You'll often see posts from parents who are recommending their nanny or looking for a nanny share, or you can post your own question.

DAYCARE BASICS

"Daycare" can mean two things: a daycare center or an at-home facility (someone's home). Home daycares are often led by a stay-at-home parent caring for other children concurrently to help manage family costs. It's also worth mentioning workplace daycares here, which fall under the banner of a "daycare center." In many cases, they're outstanding facilities—but that's not universal. These centers are sometimes run by national chains, which can be a great or not-so-great thing; evaluate them with just as selective an eye as you would any other daycare center, even if it is one hundred times more convenient than any other option.

For some families, "daycare" isn't even in their vernacular: their children go to *school*, even when as young as six weeks. For instance, Montessori programs bring structure and a learning-oriented mindset even to their infant and toddler classrooms. Many parents love having a child-development professional with their baby, which can be hard to find with a nanny. (For the sake of simplicity, I'm going to use the word "daycare" to apply to all group childcare.)

The Pros of Daycare
UNADULTERATED PROS

- There are other children to play with. That built-in socialization supports your child's brain development and eases the transition into more structured school later. One mom "worried less about arranging playdates in off-hours, because [her] child had had plenty of friend time already."

- You don't have to worry that you're wholly responsible for someone else's livelihood (as with a full-time nanny). Some daycare centers can be flexible about the number of hours used each week, so families can scale down or up (with adequate notice) without impacting someone's ability to pay her rent or mortgage.

- With a regulated, licensed facility, there are checks and balances, with oversight of the staff. Many parents appreciate knowing their childcare providers have been thoroughly vetted and are closely managed. (Note: it is *very* important that you ask questions about licensing during your screening process; you'll find a list of questions and what to look for in their answers at herestheplanbook.com.)

- Staffs have built-in extra coverage allowing breaks for caregivers. A larger staff also means that no one person is going to be alone with your child.

- Children can get out of the house for at least part of the day, and families can maintain the privacy of their home (as opposed to in-home care).

- In Montessori and other school-like childcare facilities, the childcare providers—usually professionals who've chosen childcare and education as a career path—are highly trained in child development and attuned to the developmental milestones.

- Structured facilities offer dependability—all holidays and vacation days are established in advance. At-home daycares are not foolproof; if the home daycare provider is sick, you may not have coverage that day.
- There's much less one-on-one attention, which some families prefer. One mom explained: "It's really important to me that my kids don't feel like they're the center of the world." If a teacher can't see to the baby's needs immediately, she learns how to self-soothe and develop patience. Another mother found daycare helped her clingy son become much more independent.
- Parents need to relinquish control when their child is attending daycare. "I had anxiety and control issues about getting him to sleep and how much he was eating," a social psychologist told me. "Daycare forced me to let go. And it turns out, he did just fine."

The Cons of Daycare

- Children get sick frequently in daycare: they're all in close proximity, they put everything in their mouths, and they have developing immune systems.
- You can't bring your child to daycare when sick; typically, your child must be fever-, vomit-, diarrhea-, and rash-free for twenty-four hours before returning to school.
- If you work long or unpredictable hours or travel frequently for business, finding a daycare solution can be nearly impossible. It can also be a headache if you rely on public transit.
- Again, there's much less one-on-one attention. Different states have different regulations about the ratio of adults to children, but there will often be four babies per adult. So if you have a colicky, fussy, or difficult baby who requires a lot of soothing and holding, you might worry.

Which Daycare?

- Trusted recommendations are most parents' starting point for finding the right childcare.
- Locations near home are ideal for parents who travel or sometimes work from home, and for those who don't want to subject their kids to a long commute twice daily.
- Locations near work are essential for parents who must pick up their kids from daycare soon after leaving work, as well as for breast-feeding mothers who might want to stop by during the day.

The Costs of Daycare

While "lower cost" is one of the reasons parents often cite for choosing daycare, it is still by no means inexpensive. National organizations will cite cost ranges from $350 to $1,500 per month, but those figures are typically based on statewide averages. In urban areas, those costs skew much, much higher; in New York City we saw rates in the $2,500-per-month range. Plus, in most cases you're paying year-round, even if you take your child out for vacation.

WORKING WITH A NANNY

There's a broad perception (and in some cases misconception) that only privileged people have nannies. When I was growing up, I certainly thought that; I had a college boyfriend who'd had a nanny his whole life, and it sounded almost indulgent to me. The reality, though, is that for some families it's the only tenable option.

The Pros of Nanny Care

- For many families, the biggest prime benefit is the one-on-one care a nanny provides and the flexibility that brings.
- Nannies free you from needing to shuttle your child to and fro every day. This makes nannies an excellent choice for parents who work long or unpredictable hours, travel frequently for business, or rely on public transit.

- Nannies can perform some household tasks and errands, freeing up your time before and after work.
- They can be more economical than daycare if you have more than one child.
- They can be even more economical if you go with a "nanny share" (see the "Nanny Shares" section coming up).

The Cons of Nanny Care

- It can be hard to adjust to having a paid employee handling some (or all) of your home life. One woman was deeply uncomfortable asking someone to do things for her that she was fully capable of doing herself, even if she had no time in which to do them.
- The things that make a potential nanny the perfect fit (like her being a parent as well) can also make her a complicated choice. Her family's livelihood hinges on the paycheck she's receiving from your family.
- Nannies require management, such as formalizing a contract, setting up payroll, establishing household rules, and maintaining open lines of communication and relationship. (See heres theplanbook.com for a sample nanny contract.)
- It's expensive! (See "The Costs of a Nanny" below.)
- Being the sole caretaker all day means your nanny won't get any breaks from the kids other than at naptime. If she's having an off day, there isn't anyone around to pick up the slack.
- While you'll be covered when your *child* gets sick, you're out of luck when your *nanny* gets sick.
- There's always the risk that she will resign on short notice and leave you in a bind.

These last two cons illuminate why the "Expect change!" mantra is so important: you need to be logistically ready for it, with backup plans and coverage. You also need to be emotionally prepared. When

HOW TO FIND A NANNY

There are tons of online resources at your disposal to help you find a nanny: Care.com, Sittercity, UrbanSitter, and countless local services will help you find the perfect candidate for your family.

Despite that, though, a nanny search is a sweat-inducing process. You'll hear stories of families bidding against each other for the "good" nannies, or parents poaching nannies in the playground. I know one woman who, after three months of searching, finally enrolled her daughter in daycare because she was so overwhelmed by the process. Here are some of my favorite parent hacks for finding a great full-time babysitter or nanny.

SCOUR THE LISTSERVS AND ONLINE PARENTING GROUPS. Join a local parenting group online and look for posts from parents who have "outgrown" their nanny or are moving. The ones who love their nannies are usually very invested in helping them find new employment. (Be aware, though: those parents may unconsciously gloss over "trouble" areas, so be sure to speak with past employers.)

MAKE SURE YOUR FRIENDS KNOW YOU'RE LOOKING. If they have a nanny, she could be a great source of candidates. When a close family friend had a new baby, I connected her with our nanny's niece who was looking for a job. They clicked, and it wound up being a huge win for us too: our nannies and our babies wound up spending three days a week together, and the kids became best friends.

GO LOW-TECH. Similarly to the parents who "advertise" their nanny on email Listservs, there are parents who post notices at their kids' school or community centers. One mom I interviewed said she called up the local Montessori and asked if they knew of any families' nannies looking for work. You can also ask if you can post flyers in those locations. Nannies who are dropping off and picking up often have time to linger around these bulletin boards.

WRITE AN AMAZING JOB DESCRIPTION. When posting on a site or message board, be thorough—not just about what you're looking for, but why someone would want to work for your family. Invest time in this: it'll save you a ton of time screening out people who aren't a fit, and it'll also draw more applicants. As one Microsoft manager phrased it, if you're looking for a COO for your household, say that, and sell yourselves as a supportive, nurturing, fun-loving family. (For more tips on writing a great caregiver job description, visit herestheplanbook.com.)

SET UP SOME HURDLES. When searching for candidates on a site like Care.com or even Craigslist, the challenge is to narrow a very wide pool of applicants to a manageable number. Christine Anderson, a managing director at Blackstone, has perfected this art. In her initial job post, she always asks interested candidates to respond to her post directly rather than submitting a form letter. She then focuses on the applicants who write personal responses and sends follow-up messages to a dozen or more candidates, asking them to expand on their prior experience. She'll also include questions like "Why did you leave your last role?" She uses their responses to gauge how well and thoughtfully they communicate. She'll typically do one more round of email Q&A before arranging meetings near her office. From these meetings she selects two or three candidates to meet her children.

USE A PLACEMENT SERVICE. They pre-screen and vet candidates, which many parents prefer because it can save a tremendous amount of time and anxiety. But that convenience comes with a hefty price tag: usually 10 percent (or more) of the first year's salary.

you're working with one caregiver for a year or two or more, and she's with your child for eight to ten hours a day, it—justifiably—feels like she is a partner in raising your child. It's easy to get deeply emotionally attached, and chances are, she's incredibly attached to your child as well. But at the end of the day, while she may feel like family, she's your employee, and it is a job for her.

The Costs of a Nanny

- As with daycare, costs range widely depending on where you live, but in urban areas and the suburbs surrounding them, hourly rates typically range from $15 to $19 for one child and up to $25 for three children. You'll also need to budget one to two weeks of pay for an annual bonus, and expect to offer paid vacation time.

- Should you use a placement service or agency to vet candidates, expect an additional cost of 10 percent (or more) of the first year's salary.

- There are also regulations about overtime, especially in states that have passed a Domestic Workers Bill of Rights. To save money and avoid overtime, some families keep a few on-call sitters for when they'll need more childcare than is covered in their nanny's contract.

- You'll be expected to provide an annual raise ($1/hour or $50/week per year is common); you'll also need to boost your nanny's pay if and when you have another child.

- Additional perks can add up quickly: a "metro card" for public transit, cell phone service, petty cash to cover snacks and outings with the children.

- There are nanny taxes; depending on your state, you'll pay roughly 8 percent additional in taxes, and the forms can be onerous. Use a service like Care.com's HomePay (www.myhomepay.com) to simplify nanny payroll and taxes. Note: paying off-the-books and evading those taxes can have serious financial and professional repercussions.

- While workers' compensation insurance isn't a requirement in every state, it can help insulate your family from significant financial damages (such as if your nanny were in an accident while driving your child to a playdate).

NANNY SHARE 101

With a nanny share, you and another family share the cost of a nanny, who cares for both families' children. Nanny shares are surging in popularity; Tom Breedlove from HomePay, which handles nanny payroll, told me 30 percent of their customers are families in nanny shares.

Since you should compensate the caregiver for caring for two children and managing two families, it usually winds up costing a little more than half of a typical nanny salary. Courtney Klein, founder of maternity-wear startup Storq, told me, "Nannies are expensive, but someone taking care of your child *should* be paid well." It's hard and exhausting work, and she saw joining a nanny share as a way to ensure the person caring for her child was well compensated without having to solely carry the burden of her salary.

The Pros of Nanny Shares
- You get the convenience, flexibility, and special attention of a nanny without as much sticker shock.
- Your child has a playmate.

The Cons of Nanny Shares
- Neither finding a family to nanny share with nor hiring the right nanny is easy.
- You have to accommodate the wants and needs of another family. You'll want to ensure a smooth, viable relationship between your families and with your shared nanny, which calls for additional screening and contracts.

HIRING AN AU PAIR

An au pair lives with you and is treated as a member of your family. (The name comes from the French term for "on par.") Ranging from eighteen to twenty-six years old, au pairs come to the U.S. for one year on a J-1 visa, which is, in broad terms, an educational visa that promotes cultural exchange. The program is administered by the State Department, which has designated about fifteen agencies to sponsor au pairs and facilitate their hiring. (There's a full list of them, with links, on herestheplanbook.com.) The agencies are responsible not only for matching candidates and families but also for handling all of the logistics of the au pair's travel and employment. They also educate both families and au pairs about the program and the importance of cultural exchange, as well as provide support throughout the year.

The Pros of Au Pairs
UNADULTERATED PROS

- Au pairs provide full-time childcare for considerably less than the cost of a nanny and often less than daycare as well. If you have the space (and the willingness to sacrifice some privacy), an au pair can be one of the least expensive—and most flexible—childcare arrangements you can get.
- The fifteen different au pair agencies handle much of the sourcing and screening you'd have to do yourself when hiring a nanny. Au pair candidates (and prospective host families) create extensive online profiles, including photos, essays, and videos. When you find someone who feels like a match, you conduct interviews by Skype.
- The good agencies hold your hand through the entire process, from finding the right match, to welcoming her into your home and integrating her into your family, to maintaining open lines of communication—right down to mediating any potential disagreements or misunderstandings.

CONDITIONAL PROS

- Having someone living in your home means you always have an extra adult around in a pinch. So when I was in Las Vegas on a business trip and my husband found out he needed to be in San Francisco at 8:00 AM the next day, it was no big deal because we have an au pair. That said, you also have someone else living in your home.

- Interestingly, according to the au pair agency we work with, au pairs rarely miss work on account of illness, and I've found that to be true in our family. However, because she lives with you, if your au pair *does* get sick, you'll likely be the one serving up chicken soup and TLC.

- A "bad" match (whether that's because the au pair isn't as capable as you had expected, because you're facing communications problems, or simply because she's homesick) isn't irreparable. A hands-on agency will find an alternative placement (for both her and you).

- One supposed pro often trips up families: hiring an au pair does not guarantee your child will learn a foreign language— often because au pairs want to perfect their English. Even if you're very clear about your expectations during the interview process, there's no guarantee your child will pick up some Italian or Portuguese.

The Cons of Au Pairs

- You host an au pair in your home 24/7, which exponentially increases any privacy concerns you may have.

- The State Department imposes very strict rules on how much an au pair can work: no more than forty-five hours a week, and no more than ten hours per day. So if, say, you and your spouse travel frequently, you can't have your au pair watch the kids for twenty-four hours while you're gone.

- Similarly, it's predetermined what an au pair may *not* do—like clean your house.

- As with nannies, you'll need to establish and maintain house rules.
- Au pairs must be between the ages of eighteen and twenty-six, so they're less experienced than many other childcare providers. In some cases, an au pair can seem more like another child in your home than like a capable adult.
- Au pairs are placed for one or two years maximum, requiring an additional investment of time and training should you choose to continue with the program with a new au pair.
- The application, selection, and interview process is arduous and time-consuming. (I mentioned above that au pairs write essays and make videos: you have to do the same.) And even if you find the right candidate immediately, it can still take months for her to arrive if she's coming from her home country. (Some candidates are already in the States, completing a contract with another host family.)
- The applicant pool may be shallow. There are "seasons" for au pairs, in which there's a big push of applications, and those differ country by country. You'd want to be sure you're not looking for an au pair during a "dry season."

The Costs of an Au Pair

- The all-in cost of an au pair averages $18,500 for one year. You pay an au pair's weekly stipend of about $200 (set by the U.S. State Department) directly to her; she's responsible for paying taxes on that amount. You also need to afford at least one and a half days off per week, one full weekend off per month, and two weeks of paid vacation.
- You also pay an up-front placement fee to the agency, which can vary but is generally in the $7,000 to $8,500 range. (Many will waive registration costs or give you a discount on your fee; hunt around on Google before signing up with any agencies.) That up-front fee covers costs like travel to the U.S. and health care, so it's not fully refundable if you part ways with your au pair.

- As part of the State Department program, au pairs are required to take at least six credits of classes from an accredited post-secondary school, and families are required to cover up to $500 of those educational costs.
- The cost of room and board—depending on your family and the au pair—can be either minimal or burdensome. One parent told me their male au pair was eating what seemed like hundreds of dollars' worth of groceries a week. There are also variable costs, like cell phone plans and car insurance premiums.

FAMILY CARE

When I was pregnant with my first baby I started doing the math in my head: a smallish one-bedroom apartment in my neighborhood cost around $2,500 a month, which was considerably less than the cost of a nanny and pretty much a wash with daycare (which we'd already conceded was an impossibility because of our work schedules). We could rent an apartment for my retiree parents, and *they* could take care of the baby! For less than it would cost to get a nanny! And it would be family!

I told a friend all about my grand plan, most of which amounted to not needing to "figure out" the whole childcare thing and saving money at the same time. I remember her cocking her eyebrow at me and then saying, levelly, "You think there's no cost to having your mother as your babysitter?"

I thought I'd found a brilliant solution to what seemed an intractable problem: the anxiety of turning your child over every day to someone you barely know. I hadn't really thought about what it would mean to task my sixty-year-old mother with the care of a needy baby (soon to become an active toddler) for fifty hours a week.

That's not to say that family care isn't a wonderful solution for some, but in most of the successful instances I've heard about, the family care was supplemental to a nanny or daycare. Take this example: Tracy Rahal is a corporate lawyer, and her husband, Jason, is a neurosurgeon; both of their schedules are incredibly demanding. When Jason's parents offered to help with childcare, they worked out a system that would afford Tracy and Jason the support they needed without being a huge burden to his parents. Their son went to daycare on Mondays, Tuesdays, and Fridays. On Tuesday, he'd be picked up by his grandparents, who also cared for him during the day on Wednesday and Thursday. Tracy and Jason only had to worry about daycare pickup on Mondays and Fridays, and Jason's parents had extended long weekends to themselves to travel or see their friends.

Stay-at-Home Dads

One mother I interviewed made a deal with her husband early in their relationship: "Whoever was earning the most money when the kids were born would get to keep working." Her salary won out, and her husband wound down his business over the course of her pregnancy. He's embraced his new role, but it's also given both of them a window onto the inequities of being the primary caregiver for young children.

They were living in Tribeca, and her husband spent his days on the playground with what this woman affectionately called his "daytime wives." "They were beautiful, accomplished women who'd chosen to stay home." But as a stay-at-home dad, he was much more noticeable—and often was lauded for his commitment to his children. "He'd meet someone when he was out on a stroller walk with one of these women, and he would get all these compliments." But the women he was with—professional rock stars who'd been partners at Deloitte & Touche or who had run advertising agencies—were largely ignored in these conversations. It was somehow assumed that he'd made more sacrifices than they had.

I was surprised to hear, too, that she and her husband have observed the stay-at-home dads in their orbit having the same reentry and on-ramping problems that women face when they've been out of the workforce for a couple of years. "There seems to be even *more* of a stigma," she said. "Interviewers look at you in a way that says, 'So you just hung out in the park for two years?'"

The chief compliance officer at a financial services firm told me that, in her working-class Boston neighborhood, "a stay-at-home dad is looked at like an alien." Her husband, who'd given up his architecture practice to stay home with their new baby, struggled to find a sense of community and support. She nudged him toward new-baby Meetups and Tiny Tots music classes, and he'd come home complaining that the women there were insufferable. "Men just don't want to talk about the same baby stuff that moms do," she said. "Even if they're new dads." He hated having conversations about whether their babies had taken four ounces of milk yet or how long it had been since they'd pooped. "Moms want to feel like what's going on in their lives is normal. They want a community around being a mom," she said. "He wanted a community around being a human."

That loneliness and isolation made the work of caring for a baby all day even more depleting. When his wife got home from the office, he was so spent he'd need to entirely disengage, which meant she was left fully on-duty as a solo parent until her girls went to bed. "Working dads don't walk in the door and get handed two buckets of scream," she told me. "And stay-at-home moms don't have their day end when the working dad gets home."

But, she reasoned, "I'm satisfied in my day-to-day; I'm around interesting, motivated, intelligent people." Though her husband isn't satisfied he pushes on because, in her words, "he sees it as a duty." It's a constant struggle for her to watch him suffer, but it's given her this unique perspective into the life of a stay-at-home mother. "You're constantly on call for other people, and nobody is on call for you."

And, dismayingly, the wives of stay-at-home dads get derision too. One professor told me that she went out for drinks with a few colleagues who didn't have children, and she shared her frustration that many of her students don't want to pursue PhDs because they believe you can't have an academic career and a family. "But I'm doing it!" she told her colleagues proudly. They gave her blank stares. "But you're not doing it," they said. "Your husband is a stay-at-home dad." She was floored. "I have no street cred because I haven't suffered," she told me. "Any achievement I had was 'cheating the system' because I have a supportive spouse."

But no matter the form your childcare arrangement takes, the most important takeaway for this chapter, which you've already heard more than once: expect change.

WORTH REMEMBERING

- It's never too early to start thinking about childcare, but keep an open mind about what's going to work for your family. Thoroughly consider all of the options.
- Hope for the best, but prepare for the worst. Having a backup plan for your backup plan is what's going to keep your work life going.
- Do deep research on the childcare provider you decide on: you're not just protecting your child's safety, you're also protecting your ability to focus and concentrate when you're at work.

CHAPTER 7

RETURNING TO WORK

I n researching this book I collected data and stories from more than two thousand working mothers about their experiences, anxieties, and advice. More than 70 percent of them expressed some ambivalence about returning to work, with a full 24 percent saying they weren't remotely ready. Most felt that their maternity leave wasn't long enough.

For many, this struggle is rooted in separation anxiety. Though it doesn't start to show in infants until they're at least six months old, it can hit mothers like a truck whatever the baby's age. One woman told me, "I felt like I was leaving a part of my soul at daycare every day." Another was so distraught, her husband had to do the drop-off: if she had to say goodbye at daycare, she was a wreck for the rest of the day.

But even if you don't experience separation anxiety, you still have to layer the logistical challenges of your day job on top of the immense responsibilities of caring for a newborn or infant.

It. Is. Not. Easy.

Yet many women expect they'll ramp back up to their previous capacity immediately upon walking into their office. And if they don't, they're riddled with self-doubt or disappointment. My mantra for returning to work is "manage expectations." You need to manage your colleagues' expectations of your capacity—but even more, you have to manage your own.

Cali Williams Yost, CEO and founder of Flex+Strategy Group, has coached countless women through their reentry to the office, and she likens it to a three-lane highway. "Too often high achievers see only two options: the fast lane, or stopped on the side of the road." She's seen women burn themselves out and leave the workforce entirely because they weren't willing to consider a slower lane. "It's okay to switch to the slower lane for a period of time," she said. "You just need to be aware of what the acceleration moments are."

MANAGING YOUR DAY

We've all heard the adage that when you want to get something done, ask a busy person. One woman said, "I felt like when I got back, the productivity switch was flipped on." She continued, "You know you have to leave by a certain time, so there's so much less bullshitting."

The key, though, is making sure you're spending your time on the *right* things. The director of training for a Boston school system laments not being more strategic about where she directed her energy when she returned to work. "A lot of small, menial tasks occupied too much of my time precisely because they were the easy tasks. They weren't necessarily the most meaningful to my career and career goals."

Rachael Ellison is an HR strategy consultant who works with corporations and executives. "When I'm working with new mothers," she told me, "I ask them to identify what value they bring to the table beyond being an endurance worker." Too often she hears women say things like, "I put the work in to get the job done," which may not be sustainable with a new baby at home. Articulating—even just to yourself!—what your greatest strengths are, and how those strengths differentiate you, can help you ensure you're focusing on the right things.

Fran Hauser, president of digital at Time Inc., told me about her return to work: "I became so careful and judicious about every minute of the day: how I'm spending it, whom I'm meeting with, and what I'm actually getting done." She engaged an executive coach around that time, who she believes was instrumental in helping her assimilate back into professional life. In addition to acting as an objective, experienced, zero-risk sounding board, the coach gave Fran some concrete exercises to help her prioritize her time and energy.

On a regular basis Fran would identify the two or three things she should focus on—things that would really move the needle. On Fridays she would take what the coach called "an airplane view" of the coming week, and reconcile those two or three things with what was on her calendar. She found that, 90 percent of the time, what was on her calendar didn't tie back to what she knew she should be prioritizing. "I would make a ton of changes on Friday afternoons," she said.

In addition to reflecting on your week ahead, look back at the week you've just finished. Most of us are very good at criticizing ourselves for our "failures," whether it's missing a deadline or missing a bedtime. We spend so much time thinking about everything we did *not* get done, rather than celebrating what we did get done. And usually, you've accomplished more than you think you have.

Fran also left ninety minutes in her morning schedule for her "thinking time." She explained, "Your most creative thinking is in the morning, before you start doing email and putting junk in your head." Carving out that time well in advance meant that she was able to actually keep those creative-thinking appointments two or three days a week for strategy or reflection. Fran would spend that time looking forward, asking herself: *What's next? Is there a major trend we're not paying attention to? Is there an acquisition we should be looking at?* "Otherwise," she said, "I wasn't looking forward. I was treading water."

Before she had kids, she would overprepare for every meeting, distributing an agenda in advance and then in hard copy at the start of the meeting. After returning to work, she said, "I would scratch some notes on a piece of paper. It became more about substance than form." She'd previously spent time doing things like making PowerPoint decks "look pretty," but refocused her efforts away from format and onto content.

At the beginning of her return, spending that hour a week with a coach felt indulgent, but over time she started internalizing the voice of her coach. Before making a major decision she'd ask herself, *What would MJ tell me to do?* And more often than not, she already had the answer. The repeated forced introspection that came from those coaching sessions had a lasting impact, making her more thoughtful, objective, and reasoned.

Note that Fran was prioritizing—which is very different from multitasking. "There's this relentless focus on multitasking," my friend Jenny told me, "and it's not necessarily a good thing." I'd always thought that the ability to do or think about several things simultaneously was a strength, the type of thing you'd share in a job interview. "I'm a great multitasker!" But in reality, doing several things simultaneously diminishes your performance on *everything* you're doing.

I did a group session once with a time-management expert, and he demonstrated for us exactly what happens when your brain tries to multitask. He instructed us to make three columns on a sheet of paper. In the first we were to write a letter of the alphabet, starting with *A*. In the second, we wrote a number, starting with *1*. In the third, we drew one of three shapes: a circle, a triangle, or a square. So for the first row, we filled in *A*, *1*, and a circle.

He instructed us to move on to the next row: *B*, *2*, triangle. The third row: *C*, *3*, square. Then he'd time us as we completed the sheet, all the way to *Z*, *26*, and a final triangle. Everyone in the room raced through it; the fastest time was about a minute and a half.

Then he had us do it again, but this time we completed each column in full before turning to the next. Everyone's time was *significantly* shorter; it took about 50 percent longer when we shifted from task to task. So now, think about the implications of that for your professional life, like when you move from writing an email to looking something up online to responding to a text message. Your brain has to reset and reacclimate every time you start something new—and that takes valuable processing time and energy.

Remember this when you're participating on a conference call while responding to a note from your boss while trying to finish the presentation for tomorrow's meeting and trying to schedule a playdate for your daughter via text. You can do it all, but you can't do it all at once without slowing down or messing up.

Switching back and forth between email and the rest of your work is often the biggest culprit. Many of the successful women I spoke with condense their email in-box time to discrete blocks during the day, like 9:00 AM to 10:00 AM, 1:00 PM to 2:30 PM, and 4:00 PM to 4:30 PM. The rest of the time, they're closed out of email and focused on the work at hand. In this day and age of unrelenting availability, waiting three hours to read an email can feel like you're being unresponsive, but if you make it known to your colleagues that you're not tethered to email, they'll find another way to reach you if it is truly urgent.

MANAGING YOUR NIGHTS AND WEEKENDS

Cali Williams Yost coined the term "work+life fit" because she felt the idea of work-life *balance* was unrealistic. She told me, "Most people aren't intentional about how they're getting their work done *and* being a mother." She advocates mindful and deliberate planning in order to map out how all the pieces of the puzzle fit together.

Your spouse or partner, if you have one, has a big role to play here. You're establishing patterns now about family responsibility that will impact the next eighteen years of your life. Take advantage of the blank slate you have in your early days as parents to set norms of equal division of household labor. In Chapter 5: Maternity Leave, I talked about specific ways you can do this, like the woman who with her husband created a Google calendar, assigning blocks of time to each of them. Every week, those hours needed to equal out between them—and they divvied up *every hour* that their child wasn't at daycare. It wasn't just about who was going to be home on what night, but also about who was feeding the baby breakfast and who was doing the middle-of-the-night wake-ups. One mom told me of her relationship with her wife: "We have the advantage of having no preconceived ideas about who has which 'role.'" Since neither had been socialized to think she was "better" or "worse" at baby care or wage earning, they divided things up in the way that made the most sense to them as individuals.

If you don't have a partner, lean on friends, family, neighbors—and hired help when you can afford it. Take it from Rachel Sklar, a single mother and founder of The Li.st. "Any mom knows that you learn how to do things one-handed," she told me. "That's the metaphor. Being a single mom is one-handedness. You just get good at it." She also explained that support doesn't have to come from a partner. One of her friends put together a "sleep fund" for her, which she used to hire a doula without guilt about spending money on it. Other friends drop by and lend a hand with the baby so she can get some work done. As someone who has always been independent, she's had to learn how to accept help and make the most of it. "You have to be organized about marshaling that goodwill."

According to Yost's research, 72 percent of people *think* they're being deliberate and intentional about managing their work-life day, but only 52 percent actually are. Managing your work schedule and time at the office only gets you halfway there; you also have to be mindful of all the other little details that make your home function.

One of my friends made the most of her time doing errands by turning it into one-on-one time with her toddler. "We're going on an adventure!" she'd tell him. "To the dry cleaner!" A two-year-old doesn't know that's a chore; he just knows it's time with mom focusing just on him.

For years experts have advised that buying experiences—or services—rather than things has a much more lasting impact on happiness. And when you invest in services like housecleaning or errand-running you're literally buying time for yourself. I personally call it "arbitraging my time": figuring out how much my time is worth, and off-loading the things I can hire someone to do for less money. There have been plenty of days I've hired our (willing) babysitter to help organize our apartment or run some errands for me so I could work or enjoy time with the kids. Services like TaskRabbit make it easy to find people for one-off jobs.

Lindsay Cookson is a marketing director at Dolby Laboratories. When she went back to work, she realized how much of her day was lost to mundane busyness, and how hungry she was to get that time back, even if it meant scrimping in other places. So she and her husband drafted a job description for a "family assistant" and hired someone to come over every morning for three hours. The assistant gets all of the baby's food ready for daycare, including ensuring all the bottle parts are clean, preparing baby food, and packing a bag for him. She does their laundry and grocery shopping, picks up prescriptions or dry cleaning, and tidies up the kitchen. She then prepares dinner for the family to reheat when they get home.

Fran Hauser became a master at this type of delegating. "I learned how to let go in a big way," she said, both professionally and personally. She hired a personal assistant to cover anything administrative in her life. She admits it sometimes feels like a luxury, but it takes time-consuming and mostly mindless tasks off her plate. Over the holidays, her assistant wrapped her gifts and mailed out her Christmas cards, which gave Fran that time to spend with her kids or get ahead on work.

Another reason to outsource: 65 percent of the women I surveyed reported that their to-do list kept them up at night. You're not just buying time by shedding some of the smaller responsibilities; you're buying *sleep*, and that's something many can't put a price on. And as you'll learn as you read on, sleep (or the lack thereof) has an enormous impact on your ability to function professionally.

But delegating certain responsibilities to others isn't the only way to off-load them: there's always the option of eliminating some entirely. One woman said her biggest regret during maternity leave was that she didn't "let [her] house be a little more dirty." During my maternity leave, I realized that some of the things I was sinking time into for weeSpring weren't delivering much return. After I eliminated tasks and responsibilities that were nonessential, I brought that same mindset to my personal life. If you had to eliminate half your domestic chores, ask yourself what would make the cut. Ironing clothes? Dusting quarterly instead of monthly? Hand-addressing holiday cards? Going to the car wash? No one in my family can tell the difference between the grocery store rotisserie chicken and the one I painstakingly stuffed with lemons and roasted myself. If in doubt, stop doing the time-consuming stuff and wait to see if anyone notices. (They probably won't.)

In your nonparent life, you may have had very blurred lines between your workdays and your personal time. That creep of work emails and little projects that need wrapping up can feel much more intrusive once you need to fit it around baby bedtime or a nursing session. Some women find that they don't have the same drive for evening or weekend work. One woman told me that after her baby was born her "rabid 24/7 focus on work had waned." It didn't mean that she cared less about her job, or that she wasn't as good at it—she just got more disciplined about protecting her personal life.

WORKING WITH A COACH

The term "life coach" often gets derided ("You need a coach, for your *life*?"), but a professional coach can be an invaluable sounding board as you navigate this major professional transition. However, according to Andrea Sparrey, who runs her own career coaching business, many more men hire coaches than women. She formed her company with the express intent of supporting women, and specifically targets her marketing at women, and yet two-thirds of her client base is male. She attributes this gap to many women being hesitant to invest (literally!) in their careers. "Women don't want to pay," she told me.

Often, a coach will help address a specific challenge or objective, like preparing for a big performance review or negotiating a job offer. But a coach can help with the big philosophical questions as well, like what your values are and whether your professional choices align with them. I think of coaching as therapy for your career: just as you might decide to see a therapist to talk through what you're struggling with as a new mother, you might also hire a coach to help you think through your professional priorities. And from a financial perspective, the cost is comparable.

As Andrea boiled it down, "Most of the people in your life have a stake in the decisions you make," whether it is a mentor in the office or your spouse. A coach is an objective and unbiased outsider who has worked with lots of other professionals dealing with challenges similar to yours. That broader perspective can make some of the nitty-gritty work like role-playing feel more authentic, because the coach knows the landscape well enough to truly understand how a conversation with your boss might go down. Rehearsing what you want to say (and thinking about the various scenarios that might play out) will help you feel prepared instead of nervous.

If you feel working with a coach would be constructive, ask around for recommendations. These days, with Skype and Google Hangout, your coach need not even be in your local area. There's also an online resource called In Your Corner (inyourcorneronline.com) that hosts digital coaching sessions at much lower rates than for in-person appointments.

Regardless of whether you decide to work with a coach, consider finding a "mom mentor." Look for someone who is at least a few years beyond where you are in your career who continued to work after she had children. "Let her be your Sherpa," said work-life expert Cali

Williams Yost. "If your sitter calls in sick the morning you're leaving for a business trip, and your baby is melting down because she doesn't know the backup sitter, you call your Sherpa." She's been there. Ask her to tell you everything is going to be okay—and when she does, believe her.

RECLAIMING YOUR TURF

Your first job when you get back to the office is to thank the people who covered for you. Buy them a pizza lunch, write lovely handwritten notes, bring a nice plant. Though these are small gestures, they're a way to immediately acknowledge the extra work they've done on your behalf. You can then continue to express your gratitude by periodically covering for them in return. They also have things going on in their lives, like getting to a yoga class or spending extra time with family around the holidays. Make their things possible for them the same way they made it possible for you to be with your baby.

And though most colleagues will be thrilled to hand your work back over to you, note that it's not universal. Just as you needed to be deliberate during your pregnancy about the work and projects you wanted, you also need to proactively communicate what types of projects you want now that you're back. One woman told me, "You may assume it's clear to everyone that you want your responsibilities back, but it isn't." Case in point: her colleague retained the client accounts she'd taken over during the maternity leave, and, worse, her boss condoned it.

"Ramping up has been a slow process," one woman lamented. "Because I'm working on a big project that's a few months out, my days weren't immediately filled. I've definitely lost some crucial relevance."

If you do project-based work, you may find you need to elbow your way back in. One lobbyist told me, "My company did a terrible job reintegrating me." They simply weren't assigning her work; she was billing only 30 percent of the time she'd been billing previously. She attributes that to her boss not going to bat for her, and she regrets not standing up for herself. "In hindsight," she said, "I should have been in their face saying, 'Give me work! Give me work!'" But her twins were just twelve weeks old, and she just didn't have the energy. "By the time I was really paying attention, it was too late."

She was laid off, and in her exit interview her company acknowledged she had been lost in the shuffle. She didn't think it had been intentional, but she recognizes now that she had needed to do more to align herself with the right people in the company, people who had the authority to assign her work.

Others were especially proactive about reintegrating with their office. "When I got back, I made sure I jumped right in," an attorney told me. "I didn't wait for permission." She sat down with the partners at her firm and said, "Here are the three things I want to do in the next quarter. How can we make this happen?" Get specific about your objectives: speak up about what you need to do to grow your career.

And document all these conversations. After you've said, "I'd like to be in the mix on X, Y, and Z projects," send a follow-up email saying that you're excited to be working on those projects—and ask about next steps.

On the other end of the spectrum, I talked to women who returned from a maternity leave on which they'd had light coverage— or none at all!—to face the mountain of work that had amassed in their absence. And while some found it a welcome distraction from missing their baby, others were just plain discouraged by the onslaught.

As to how you will fare when you're back in the office, it's easy to get mired in anxiety and fear about how you'll handle it, but those feelings are much like those you have when starting a new job. Anyone who has weathered transitioning into a new role for which she felt totally overwhelmed and underprepared knows that those feelings dissipate with time and practice. Returning from having a baby isn't much different. Being a working parent is simply a new role; you've taken on a whole new set of responsibilities that you now need to fit together with your old job.

SETTING BOUNDARIES

Signaling both "I'm committed to my job!" and "I have established boundaries!" at the same time is far easier said than done. Nearly everyone I talked to expressed that they struggle with setting professional boundaries. Work inevitably bleeds over into family time—and even if they're able to securely compartmentalize their time with their children, they're still back online after putting the kids to bed.

One woman told me, "I feel like I need to put up an away message with an apology for not responding from Friday night until Monday morning. What I need to stay sharp during the week is to unplug and be with my family on the weekends." In some cases, as in the midst of closing a deal, she'll explain to her colleagues explicitly that she'll be unreachable, telling them, "I'm doing this in part because I want to encourage you to do this as well."

"I leave at 6:00 PM," one woman told me, "but it isn't easy." She explained that she felt like she was sauntering past junior people who she knew would be there later, but she just had to get over it. "Pulling the cord and walking out is tough. Even after six years of doing it."

Women have told me that they can feel the resentment emanating from their colleagues. Sometimes the women are just projecting, but at other times there's no mistaking the message. "People think I am living it up," one adoptive mother told me, "because I leave at 5:00 PM." She's the only one on her team who has children, and she's been the recipient of passive-aggressive comments about not answering emails on Sundays, and more overt comments like "You chose to be a parent." "I was prepared for intrusive questions about how much I 'paid' for my baby," she said, "but I was totally unprepared for a comment like that." More than a year later, she's still wondering what she could have or should have said.

Michelle Muller was working for an international hotelier when she got pregnant with her first baby. Her boss would come in between 9:00 AM and 10:00 AM, and then he'd stay until 8:00 PM. "He liked having time after the phone stopped ringing to work together one-on-one." Before returning from maternity leave, she sent him an email saying that needed to change. She explained that she'd be arriving by 8:00 AM, but needed to leave at 5:00 PM. She was surprised by how receptive he was, and noted that being confident and straightforward was the key. "The more firm I was," she said, "the more respectful he was. If he sensed any weakness, he'd push back."

But boundaries aren't just about getting your boss to be flexible with a different schedule. Sometimes you have to force yourself to work in ways that don't come to you naturally. A nonprofit executive told me, "I'm at my most productive between 4:00 PM and 6:00 PM." But now that she has a baby, and she needs to pick up her daughter from daycare at 5:30, she can no longer leverage that afternoon energy surge to cruise through projects. "It's just so frustrating that I can never take full advantage of that period where I know I do my best work. I was hoping maybe I would adapt, but it hasn't happened yet."

When attorney Jennifer Hill returned to her firm, she was unapologetic about her hours. She decided that she was going to limit her in-office workday to 9:00 AM to 5:00 PM, and she wasn't going to feel guilty about it. "I focused on making every minute in the office count." She told a colleague, "You can schedule a conference call for 10:00 at night, but don't set one for 5:30 PM."

Kristen Morrissey Thiede had her three children while working in big jobs at Google. She told me, "My joy is walking my kids to school. My son holds my hand. We walk six blocks, and it's my favorite fifteen minutes of the day." After she drops him off she goes home, picks up her daughter, and they do the same thing.

One morning she had a breakfast meeting scheduled and had to have her sitter take her kids to school. While she was waiting, she learned the person she was meeting wasn't going to make it. She was furious with him, but more so with herself. "I set a boundary," she said, "and I crossed it myself." The person she was meeting had no way of knowing how important her mornings were to her. She had to take ownership of her priorities. "Everyone has their thing," she said.

"You have to figure out what it is and protect it." (And note: your thing doesn't have to be related to your children.)

She wasn't the only woman who cited mornings as sacrosanct; several told me that their babies are happiest in the mornings, so that's when they've made room for extra one-on-one time with them. "It feels more like quality time then," one explained to me. "On the weekends, it's nonstop and I feel like there are no breaks, but when I have two hours in the morning with her, it's joyful." There's also less pressure to "do": do bath time, do dinner, do bedtime; mornings feel more like family time.

Another important consideration when thinking about your time with your baby: their natural biorhythms. If you're a working parent who arrives home at 6:00 PM, it's *hard* to put your baby down in a crib an hour later and walk away. Dr. Janet Kennedy, the NYC Sleep Doctor, explained to me that 7:00 PM is when babies get their surge of melatonin. If they're awake past that surge, they'll get fussy because their bodies have released adrenaline to help them cope with being overtired—but many parents misinterpret those cries to mean the baby wants to be with the parents. It's a vicious cycle that often results in an unnecessary middle-of-the-night wake-up due to residual adrenaline. Loading up on quality time in the morning can help mitigate that abbreviated time at night.

In her book *I Know How She Does It: How Successful Women Make the Most of Their Time*, Laura Vanderkam writes about the "split shift." Women will leave their office at a "reasonable" time, like 5:00 or 5:30, have dinner with their children, and tuck them into bed. Then they're back online, doing whatever they didn't have time for before they left. There's a real benefit to this approach in that you get home while your children are still awake and can spend time with you—but there's a cost as well. "It impacts my marriage," one woman told me. "We spend a lot of time sitting next to each other, but we're not talking." Another said that her sleep quality has suffered; since she's plugged in until 11:00 PM, her brain is still reeling when she needs to be falling asleep.

In my own life, I've always prioritized quality over quantity. I launched a startup when my son was one and a half, and I had a second baby a little over a year after that. Usually the kids and I have one or two hours together a day on weekdays, and that's been a conscious choice. I can try to spend three hours with them, neurotically checking my smartphone every ten minutes, which generally leaves me feeling I haven't connected with my kids. Or I can unplug for an hour, and really give them my attention and focus. I choose the latter.

MAINTAINING YOUR PRIVACY

Insulating your personal life from your professional obligations is important, but so is the converse: keeping your personal life from bleeding into your work life. One woman told me, "If I could do it over, I wouldn't have my babysitter email me at my work email." It sounds simplistic, but the core message of a choice like that is that your work persona can get easily taken over by your mom persona. "Having conversations about your kid's sleep schedule over the cubicle wall just isn't smart," she said. It's less about your interaction with that individual than about the signals you might be unwittingly sending to everyone else around you about your priorities and what's on your mind during the day.

I'm not saying not to talk about your kids at work, but be intentional about what you're saying and when. Don't use your baby as the fodder for idle chatter. Replacing "I can't believe it's still raining!" with "I was up all night with a teething baby!" can pigeonhole you into the mommy box, and that box is *very* hard to climb out of. You need to mindfully avoid the stigma of being perceived as overwhelmed, juggling too much, or prioritizing your home life at the expense of your work.

A Wall Street communications director told me: "I don't spend a lot of time telling my colleagues about the ugly underbelly of what it means to be a working mother." That conscious and careful separation of home life and work life hasn't gone unnoticed; her boss remarked once that he appreciates that she doesn't bring into the office the drama that goes on at home. "They don't know that there was a poop explosion when I was on a conference call," she said. "I don't spend time telling them how badly I slept. If someone says they had a rough night, I don't say, 'Well you should see how I sleep!'"

Now, of course you'll need to vent. Everyone needs to vent. But email your new-parent group about your colicky baby, or text your sister your story about getting pooped, peed, and puked on all in the span of one hour. *Don't* bring it up with your boss's executive assistant.

THE GUILT TRAP

Filmmaker Lacey Schwartz told me how relieved she was to find that she still found her work fulfilling after having a baby. She likened her anxiety to fear of having a lobotomy: "It was so disconcerting to me when everyone told me that I'd find a higher purpose after having a baby. I was worried I'd wake up and not care anymore about the things I used to care about." Fortunately, it turned out that adding a sense of purpose as a parent didn't disrupt the sense of purpose she derived from making films.

That said, I don't know any working moms who don't grapple with guilt. They feel like they're neglecting their child when they're at work, and they feel like they're neglecting their work when they're with their child. They also panic about what it means to let their home life bleed over into their work life. Do their colleagues see that as indicating they're not working as hard? (Interestingly, they're less worried about their superiors than about their peers or direct reports.) One woman told me she worries: "Are they going to find out that when I was working at home, I played with my baby between 10:30 AM and 10:50 AM?" She was working from 7:30 PM to 9:30 PM after her baby was in bed, so she more than made up for any breaks during the day, but she was still stricken with guilt.

"Comparing yourself to someone else is *never* a happy thing to do," one woman said. "No one else's marriage is like yours, no one

else's economic situation is like yours. You just have to let it go."
Another talked about "the sacrifice Olympics of modern parenting":
who is giving up more, who is working harder. One entrepreneur
told me her mantra was "Motherhood, not martyrdom."

"Some days I am a great mom. Some days I am a great doctor. They are
never the same day."

—AN ER RESIDENT IN ATLANTA

Brace yourself now for commentary about your choice to work,
particularly as it pertains to who cares for your baby during the day.
This kind of commentary has ignited the so-called mommy wars, and
there's little you can do to stop it.

You'll hear things like:

- "I just can't imagine who would be watching my baby if I wasn't."
- "Who do you want raising your children? Your daycare or you?"
- "We didn't try so hard to have a baby to just hand him off to
  someone else to raise."

My only advice is to not engage, assume best intentions, and just
shrug off what you can. I haven't yet found a retort that squashes the
conversation or magically injects empathy into the other person. I've
engaged in more online flame wars than I'd care to admit with people
who feel there's only one way to raise a child, and those wars haven't
done much other than raise my blood pressure. One mom told me she
tries to remind herself that all parents (including her) are doing the
best they can. "I am modeling to my daughter what a strong, independent, successful woman looks like."

And take note: there may come a point when you start to question whether it's worth it—whether you should quit work because you
can't be great at both your career and parenting. "That is a day," one
woman advised, "for a glass of wine, not rash decisions."

When everything feels like too much, scale back on the things that aren't true priorities. You have to start first by acknowledging what those priorities are (your health, your baby, your marriage, your job) and strip away everything else. "Do not plant a huge vegetable garden that summer," an HR manager said. "Don't volunteer to make 250 invitations for your sister's wedding." You don't have to join the company's every-Thursday-night volleyball league; just show up once in a while to have a beer with the team.

I urge you to think long and hard before making a decision to go part-time. One woman said, "You keep all of the responsibility, but get less pay." Others warned that you're painting yourself into the mommy box, and that it's hard to stay top-of-mind with colleagues as someone whose career is on the way up. Cali Williams Yost advised that if you want or need to reduce your hours, make it for a discrete period of time, like working four days a week for the six months after you return from maternity leave. If you need a more lasting arrangement, she advocates working full-time but with flexibility on where and when you get your job done. "Put together a program for yourself and propose it," she said. "Explain when you'll be in the office, how much work you'll do at home, and how you'll keep lines of communication open in that time."

Be aware that you may have to work especially hard in those at-home hours to stay top-of-mind with your colleagues. For example, I heard from one Los Angeles–based woman who started working two days a week from home after her first child was born. She'd made the shift after the company hired a new boss for her who lived in Portland, Oregon, and spent three days a week in Los Angeles. "No one made comments about him being in Portland on Mondays and Fridays," she told me, "but they'd refer to me as working part-time or job-sharing." Since she saved herself a couple of hours a day in commuting time— not to mention sparing herself the office chitchat that can eat up a day—she got even more work done than she had before her leave. But her colleagues had jumped to conclusions because she'd just had a baby. So she kept her head down, got her work done, and seized an opportunity elsewhere when it came her way.

LOOKING GOOD, FEELING GOOD REDUX

Rachel ten Brink, a former beauty exec who now runs a fragrance startup, talked about the "disposable clothing stage." In those early postpartum months, when you can't cope with continuing to wear your old maternity clothes and can't yet fit into your real clothes, you can start to feel a real sense of despair: "I was in Old Navy clothes all the time," she said. "I thought, *If I buy another Old Navy sweatshirt, I'll die.*" But the sweatshirt phase works only when you're staying at home; getting out of the house when you feel horrible about how you look is immeasurably harder.

You'll hear that breast-feeding can burn up to six hundred calories in a day, but that's a dramatic oversimplification of what's going on in your body after childbirth. In fact, the elevated prolactin that stimulates milk production can also reduce your metabolism.[9] Your weight—and the way your body processes and stores energy—is also tied to your thyroid function (up to 10 percent of women develop hypothyroidism post-birth, which causes weight gain); how much of the stress hormone cortisol you have coursing through your body; and your levels of sleep deprivation (less sleep = less weight loss).

All of that taken together means it may take longer than you expect to get back to looking—and feeling—like yourself. And though it can certainly feel like it, whether or not you fit in your jeans isn't a reliable metric of success in parenthood *or* your professional life.

How you look on the surface (and how you feel underneath) also impacts how others perceive you. As one woman told me, "I don't want to be the frazzled new mom. I want to be the woman who has her shit together."

The other side of that, though, is the effort and time that get sunk into your appearance. "There's a lot of upkeep for a working woman," one mother lamented. "Manicures, pedicures, waxing, hair."

PRO TIPS FOR LOOKING LIKE A PRO

Pulling on your black maternity pants *yet again* for work, six months postpartum, is just plain demoralizing. Bolstering your confidence by feeling good about how you look goes a long way, especially when you're otherwise feeling a little vulnerable. Here are the best tips I heard:

ESTABLISH A UNIFORM THAT'S MACHINE-WASHABLE AND INTER-CHANGEABLE, AND THEN MIX IT UP WITH ACCESSORIES. In those early transition months back to work, you won't have to think about what you'll be wearing. (Both Mark Zuckerberg and Barack Obama have publicly spoken about how they wear the same thing every day so they have one less choice to make.)

USE TECH HACKS TO REMEMBER WHAT LOOKS GOOD TOGETHER. Snap photos of outfits you like in order to make putting together an outfit extra easy.

DRESSES ARE YOUR FRIENDS. The right cut, fabric, and color can be incredibly forgiving—as well as versatile. I like a navy or black empire waist or wrap with a deep V in matte jersey; it'll hold up great in the wash and won't cling to any bumps or lumps.

INVEST IN SOME NURSING TOPS OR DRESSES IF YOU'LL BE BREAST-FEEDING AFTER YOU RETURN TO WORK. Companies like Japanese Weekend Maternity make nursing dresses that you'd never be able to differentiate from a "normal" dress, but they have discreet pockets that make it easy to pump without having to strip naked.

KEEP A BOUNCY SEAT IN YOUR BATHROOM SO YOU CAN MAKE TIME TO BLOW-DRY YOUR HAIR. It sounds silly, but there's a reason entire chains of blow-dry salons have popped up across the country: women feel more confident when their hair looks like someone spent some time and energy on it.

ASK YOUR HAIRSTYLIST TO SHOW YOU A QUICK-AND-EASY PROFESSIONAL-LOOKING UPDO. This is for the days when the above tip is an impossibility. You're looking here for an alternative to a messy ponytail that you can still pull off with minimal effort.

STOCK YOUR OFFICE WITH BACKUPS. You want backup shoes for when yours are uncomfortable, a backup top if you leak or have a pumping spill, and backup (costume) jewelry for the many, many times you'll walk out of the house without it.

BUY A SALON CAPE just like the one you wear during a haircut. Wear it over your work clothes in the morning after you get dressed, and take it off just before you walk out the door. It's like a reverse superhero cape: you wear it at home so you can look great without it.

INSTALL A FULL-LENGTH MIRROR RIGHT BESIDE YOUR DOOR AT HOME, and do a front-and-back check both before you put on your coat *and* after.

She asked me, very seriously, how others made time for it; she felt like there's an enormous amount of peer pressure to look polished. She confessed that she sometimes schedules meetings over manicures, if she knows the other person really well. "It just seems more productive than talking over coffee."

WORKING FROM HOME

Fun fact: new research has shown that when employees are given the option to work from home, they are *more* productive. In 2013, Stanford professor Nicholas Bloom conducted an experiment with Chinese travel website Ctrip that saw higher engagement and better results from the team members who worked from home. In addition, the company saved almost $2,000 per employee in less than a year.[8]

WARDROBE MALFUNCTIONS, NEW-MOTHER STYLE

When futurist and author Amy Webb made her first on-stage appearance after her baby was born, she was *ready*: she pumped right before taking the stage, and made sure she had tucked nursing pads into her bra. While energetically pacing the stage delivering her talk, she started to hear a swishing sound. "It wasn't my shoes," she said. "And it wasn't my dress." When she glanced at one of the enormous screens projecting her image, she saw that one of her nursing pads had been creeping out of her bra and past the neckline of her dress—until it became lodged under her clip-on microphone. "That was fifteen minutes into my hour-long presentation," she said.

While on a flight to an important event, an attorney (with a four-month-old baby at home) was seated in the vicinity of several infants. Their cries at takeoff and landing triggered her letdown—she leaked through both her nursing pads *and* her dress. Having no choice but to race to her event straight from the airport, she spent the rest of the day and evening with her arms crossed over her chest.

She wasn't the only woman I spoke with who ran into trouble on an airplane. One writer, seated between two men and unable to sneak away to pump, noticed her button-down shirt straining as her breasts became engorged. After a couple of hours, the gap between buttons had become a gaping hole. (Take this as a cautionary tale! If you wear a button-down for easy-access pumping, make sure it's roomy.)

Lynn Perkins, the founder of UrbanSitter, told me about feeling so pleased with herself one day for making it to the office early enough to stop at Starbucks. While she waited in line, a man tapped her on the shoulder to tell her she had something on her coat. She'd trailed a bright yellow bib—stuck with Velcro to her wool jacket—all the way to downtown San Francisco. The bib read: "In trouble? Call 1-800-GRANDMA."

This jump in efficacy has a couple of key underpinnings. First, you're eliminating commuting time. According to the U.S. Census Bureau, the average commute time in the United States is 25.4 minutes—which means that people who work from home get *an extra hour* in their day every day. Second, you're reducing distractions, like the coworker who swings by your desk to chat; Bloom calls this the "cake in the break room effect." One woman told me, "When I work from home, I am far more productive than at the office where I am repeatedly interrupted—and guilty of interrupting myself—by others. . . . I can get a ton more done in a much shorter time."

That said, as a working parent, there are distractions aplenty in your own home. (Kids! Dirty dishes! The cable guy!) "Especially if you're an OCD type who likes lots of order," one woman told me, "it's so difficult to reframe your brain to *not* see the house as something that needs constant management. I am constantly laying down boundaries around what I can and can't do during my workday at home." You have to be able to let go of the dirty dishes in the sink or the LEGOs strewn around the living room, and not everyone can do that.

One small step toward establishing a boundary between family work and professional work: getting dressed. That might mean putting on a dress and makeup, or it might just mean a shower and jeans. One woman told me, "I change into 'work pajamas' to shift into work mode."

Childcare is an absolute necessity, whether it's dropping your baby at daycare or having a nanny in your home. If your child is at home, a short break from working at home—the same time you'd take to run out for a coffee at the office—is a chance to squeeze in some quality time. One enormously successful TV producer told me, "I promise myself two hours behind a closed door, followed by an hour of doing 'home stuff' like playing with my kids or organizing a million things I should have done a month ago like preschool applications or doctor appointments or . . . well, napping." When that hour is up, she goes back to diligent, focused work behind closed doors.

Amanda Clayman, a well-known financial therapist, uses the Pomodoro Technique to stay on-task when working from home. Named for the tomato-shaped kitchen timer, Pomodoro espouses twenty-five-minute distraction-free work sessions, with short breaks between. And there are *some* work tasks and household tasks that can be combined: filmmaker Lacey Schwartz likes to fold laundry while on conference calls; I like to prep dinner and chop vegetables if I have a call that doesn't require me to be in front of a computer or take notes. (Invest in a good Bluetooth headset; I like the dancing-Madonna style with a padded mic on a boom, so you sound clear and close to the phone.)

For many, routine is key: "If I don't follow a routine, the day can get squandered," an entrepreneur explained. "I've found when I stick to a regular routine, I get stuff done." Academic Jenny Cookson told me that, after dropping her kids at daycare, she heads home, fills her coffee mug, then turns on her computer. "It's forward motion to the office from the second I leave the kids at school," she said. "There's no possibility for getting distracted or sucked into tidying up."

Katharine Zaleski is the founder of PowerToFly, a successful startup that matches mothers who want to work remotely with the companies that want to hire them—and she herself primarily works from a home office. Her advice: "Get out of the house every day with exercise, walks, and me time."

All of this advice applies whether you're working from home full-time, working from home one or two days a week, or working from home only when you have an emergency. And when you're deciding which of those three camps you fall in (or *want* to fall in), get introspective. Will you be able to shut the door and ignore the pile of dishes on the kitchen counter, or will it make you crazy to have that mess lurking outside your workspace? Do you have any concerns about more of the household responsibilities sliding onto your plate because you're in the house? Are you able to get the human contact you need from friends, neighbors, and your kids, or do you need to have casual interactions with your colleagues to feel connected? Because this is not just about whether working at home works for *work*; it's also about whether it works for *you*.

DEALING WITH THE UNEXPECTED

A marketing director at a tech company told me that what she was most unprepared for was "the unexpectedness of having a baby." There are countless things that can completely throw off your day: a sick baby who can't go to daycare, a babysitter with a broken-down car, a baby with an ear infection who has to go to the doctor, a daycare snow day—the list goes on.

I've heard two very polarized perspectives on how to handle these "oh crap" moments:

1. "You put it out in the open! By being authentic, you're helping shape a company culture that makes room for family life."
2. "You never use family as an excuse, unless it is a true emergency. It's no one's business."

Neither is a really good answer. (Note: there's no good answer, except to try to keep it from happening by having a backup to your backup for backup childcare.)

The problem with the first option, in my view, is that it's really hard to move the needle culturally unless you're at the top level of an organization. A Google employee told me that YouTube CEO's Susan Wojcicki's transparency about her family life was a beacon for women working for her. If she was taking her son to the doctor, her appointment calendar—viewable by any employee—would say that. Being transparent about your own personal life empowers other people to do the same. But if you're a midlevel employee at an old-school corporation, you're broadcasting that the company doesn't always come first. Of course, you want to be honest with your close colleagues, but you've got to remember that they might have an inner monologue that isn't as forgiving and understanding as what they say aloud to you. They could be wondering: *Is this going to happen a lot?* (Or worse, *Why is this happening so much?*)

For example, a senior team member at a high-profile startup had to scramble for last-minute childcare when her baby's nanny rushed to the ER, forcing her to cancel several meetings with men in her company with whom she didn't have close relationships. She polled a few male friends to get their input on how to handle it; the general tenor of their collective response was that a dad stepping in when something like this happened was viewed as a super dad, but a mom stepping in raised questions about focus and commitment—especially in the long term.

When you're dealing with someone who isn't a close colleague, one woman advised, be apologetic but vague. "I've had an unavoidable conflict come up. I apologize for the short notice. Can we reschedule for _____?"

Amanda Steinberg is the CEO and founder of the DailyWorth. "I enjoy owning the truth about kid-related interruptions," she said. "You don't have to be effusive." She can't say for certain whether she's lost deals or respect for being honest about kid stuff, but she believes that understanding and respecting family is the future of what women leaders look like. "If they're uncomfortable, it's only because they don't understand how to navigate these issues. You're here to help them."

That said, she rarely has to be honest and forthcoming about these things, because she keeps a deep list of backup helpers.

LIFE ON THE ROAD

A senior New York–based tech executive told me how she flies to California once or twice a month, which makes for a grueling forty-eight hours of air travel and meetings. "I catch a 6:00 AM flight from JFK, which means I have a 4:00 AM wake-up." She gets to San Francisco at 9:30 AM, has a full day of meetings, dinner with a colleague, and then a breakfast the next morning at 7:15 AM before heading to the

California office. "I work all day, and then catch the red-eye so I can get home before the kids leave for school."

Others affirmed this strategy for overscheduling your days when you're on the road, to maximize on that time away from your family. "I'll go to a city where I have a lot of business, and I pack my days full of meetings," a consultant told me. "Because I have this goal of squeezing in eight meetings, I wind up asking people for meetings whom I might otherwise hesitate to reach out to." This approach forces her to be proactive and disciplined about building her network. She also uses the halo effect of a speaking engagement or a big meeting to secure a sit-down with others: "I'm in town for a meeting with [important person]; do you have time to meet?"

But while she'll take a meeting on a lark if she's already scheduled to be in another town, being a mother has pushed her to get choosy about what she'll plan to leave town for. She declines conferences that she would have attended before her daughter was born. "You have to be strategic, and just think about what's worth hiring a sitter for."

Saying "no" gets hard, though, if in your mind you're passing on an opportunity because you're a mom. Morra Aarons-Mele, founder of Women Online, advised channeling someone really strong whom you admire for these moments. "Tell yourself you're saying 'no' because you're in demand, and emotionally separate it from saying 'no' because of your kids." And definitely don't tell *others* you're declining for family reasons. "That might not be feminist," Morra said, "but I'm not a believer in letting people see me sweat about being a mother."

Several women told me that every month they sit down with their spouses and match up their calendars. "I'm traveling this day, you're traveling this day," the conversations go. "This is when we'll need the nanny."

And that planning and juggling can lead to a lot more *no*'s to be conveyed to colleagues and clients. One lawyer told me she'd simply decline by saying, "I have a lot of commitments," then pass the opportunities to junior associates at her firm. For example, when she was invited to participate on a panel, she'd say, "Person X would be great for this." In doing so she made a potential negative a double positive: even though her primary objective was to pass off the responsibility, she came off as a savvy delegator who showed leadership in mentoring other women at the firm.

BREAST-FEEDING AND WORKING

I'm not going to wax poetic here about the wonders of breast-feeding. (There *are* wonders! It can be magical and blissful. You should definitely try to do it, if you can. But if you can't, you'll get no judgment from me.)

Breast *pumping*, though, is another story entirely. But in most cases, especially at the beginning, pumping while at work is what allows you to continue breast-feeding when you're with your baby. (You need to do it to maintain your supply, and also not to explode.) Pumping also, obviously, produces milk that you can give to a caregiver to feed your baby, which for some women mitigates their anxiety about being separated from their baby. There's some consolation in pumping, like, *If I can't be with my baby, at least I can do this for her.*

I started back at work on the first day of a company off-site meeting, and I had to have an uncomfortable conversation with a couple of twenty-three-year-old guys about needing space to pump. They were lovely and helpful, but I could tell from their faces that they were a little freaked-out—and that's pretty much the norm except among other mothers who've pumped in an office.

"Carrying the breast-pump bag made me feel like I was walking around with an asterisk," one woman told me. There is an upside to that easily identifiable black tote with the zippers down the front: it identifies a member of the sisterhood of nursing mothers. But from a practical perspective, feeling an occasional sense of camaraderie doesn't make the logistics any easier.

A SNEAK PEEK INTO YOUR PUMPING LIFE

"Breast-feeding is practically a full-time occupation," one woman shared. You're feeding your baby eight to ten times a day, for thirty minutes each time. In the early days after I returned to work, and I was sitting demoralized at my desk with a noisy, uncomfortable machine attached to my torso, I wrote down my schedule in a notebook:

6:00 to 6:30 AM	Wake up and get dressed.
6:30 to 7:00 AM	Feed the baby.
7:00 to 8:00 AM	Play with the baby.
8:00 to 8:15 AM	Transition with the nanny.
8:15 to 9:00 AM	Commute.
9:00 to 10:00 AM	Catch up on email.
10:00 to 10:30 AM	Pump.
10:30 AM to noon	Meetings.
Noon to 12:30 PM	Wolf down lunch.
12:30 to 1:00 PM	Pump.
1:00 to 3:00 PM	Catch up on work.
3:00 to 3:30 PM	Pump.
3:30 to 5:00 PM	Dash through a little more work.
5:00 to 5:45 PM	Commute home.
5:45 to 6:00 PM	Transition with the nanny.
6:00 to 6:30 PM	Feed the baby.
6:30 to 7:00 PM	Play with the baby.
7:00 to 7:30 PM	Give the baby a bath.
7:30 to 8:00 PM	Feed the baby again, and put him to bed.
8:00 to 10:00 PM	Do the work I didn't have time to do during the day, while eating takeout.
10:00 to 10:30 PM	Pump.
10:30 to 11:00 PM	Get pump parts ready for work the next day, and tidy up.
11:00 PM	Go to bed.

"The minute-by-minute planning is such a lonely process," one woman told me. "There are all these managerial elements, like where to put the pump when you have a client meeting after work, or how the breast milk is going to stay cold during that cocktail reception."

One of the women I interviewed told me, "Pumping is the dominant definition of my day." Another said, "I'm an accomplished person. My understanding of my world was that I could do anything I put my mind to"—and yet she struggled for months with breast-feeding.

I felt like I was doing long division in my head all day long: *If I pump at 10:30 AM, then I can make the 12:30 PM to 1:30 PM meeting because I can wait to pump until 1:30 PM. But then I've got to pump at 4:00 PM, because otherwise I won't get the fifteen ounces I need for tomorrow.* But even when you make a schedule and a plan like this, there will always be last-minute things that throw everything askew.

It's worse if you have to travel, or don't work regularly in an office. "I've pumped in taxi cabs, in an airplane seat, everywhere you can imagine," one woman said. "There's nothing more sad and lonely than sitting in a dirty place pumping with a machine when you want to be with your baby."

Cruelly, stress and anxiety make it even more difficult to pump. When you're nursing, your body has what's called a "letdown": your brain gets the message that it's time to release milk. Oxytocin is the neurotransmitter that sends that signal; it's sometimes called "the love hormone." But when you're stressed and your cortisol (another hormone) level rises, it blocks oxytocin from binding with the receptors in your brain. No oxytocin, no letdown. More than once, I found myself attached to my pump, miserably watching as *nothing happened.* It's horrible.

Some women were completely unable to produce milk if they tried to work and pump at the same time, or saw their yields radically diminished if pumping while multitasking. "I had a choice between pumping for twenty minutes and getting six ounces while working," one said, "and pumping for fifteen minutes and getting ten ounces while watching videos of my baby." Another, who surreptitiously watched episodes of *Gilmore Girls* so she could relax enough to get a letdown, wrote, "Feeling guilty about my milk supply was worse than feeling guilty about workday Netflixing."

All of this is to say: you're not alone if you're struggling. We've all heard that breast is best, but that's only true until it isn't. There is a crippling amount of social pressure to breast-feed, but the jury is still out on whether or not there's a measurable difference in outcomes for breast-fed versus formula-fed babies. Because you can't ethically tell a woman not to breast-feed, there's no way to collect controlled data. As many scientists have pointed out, the act of *choosing* to breast-feed can be as much of an indicator as the actual content of the breast milk.

Jenny Cookson, a PhD candidate and academic editor who nursed her first child for six months and her second for five weeks, said, "I am so happy I relieved myself of that particular gendered burden." She continued, "A happy mom is ultimately the best 'sustenance' for baby." If breast-feeding or pumping makes you miserable, either because you hate it physically or it's interfering with your ability to do your job, give yourself permission not to do it. Doing what's good for you will be good for the baby.

I'm not taking a position here on whether or not you should breast-feed when you go back to work; I'm simply saying it's a very personal decision that's been hijacked as a political one. People feel perfectly comfortable asking you whether you're breast-feeding, or how long you plan to breast-feed, and it foists pressure on women to— in some cases—subjugate their own health and well-being. Katherine McCleary, a teacher in Chicago, told me, "I had a breast-feeding-zealot friend who talked about formula in a tone akin to feeding your baby gasoline." Another woman, Kristen, attended a parenting class before her baby was born, and all the instructor talked about was breast-feeding. Kristen had known since she was a teenager that she wouldn't be able to breast-feed because of a physical issue; she raised her hand and asked, "What do I do when I have to formula-feed a baby?" She told me, "There was dead silence. Everyone in the class turned and stared." The teacher told her, "You *need* to breast-feed."

Women will go to crazy lengths to satisfy the "shoulds" they're hearing around them or in their own heads: you *should* be able to breast-feed without pain, you *should* nurse your baby for twelve months, you *should* be able to lose weight while nursing because you're burning six hundred extra calories a day. (As I noted earlier, recent research has indicated that, for some women, the opposite is true: they gain weight because their bodies respond to prolactin by storing fat.[10]) *You should be breast-feeding your baby* is at the core of so many of these statements, and it's so pervasive that women who cannot breast-feed, or have simply chosen not to, feel incredible shame. One woman told me she got so tired of feeling people staring at her as she assembled a formula bottle that she started sneaking off to mix bottles in a bathroom stall.

One woman confessed to me, "I was a terrible pumper." She would sit in her office's pumping closet and cry, because nothing would come. She loved breast-feeding, but felt like a total failure. "When my pediatrician told me I had to supplement with formula, I sobbed." She also compulsively apologized to people when they saw her feed her baby with formula, even without any prompting.

It doesn't have to be an all-or-nothing thing; one woman said, "I wish I'd known I could scale back, and I didn't *have* to pump three times a day at the office." Others shared similar stories about gradually introducing some formula so they could reduce the amount of time they spent pumping at work. If you have a solidly established milk supply (usually at least six months into breast-feeding), you may even be able to nurse only when you're with your baby, and have your caregiver feed her formula.

I mentioned in chapter 2 that you should ask about pumping

facilities before you go out on leave, so if they're inadequate, your employer has time to come up with something better. Your employer is required to provide a private space where you can pump that is *not* a bathroom. You need a door that locks, and it can't have glass walls. (You would think that would be a given, but no.) For more must-haves and nice-to-haves, check out the "Pumping-at-Work Basics" sidebar.

I heard from one woman who spent her first few weeks miserably pumping in a little-used bathroom. "Another—more assertive—woman returned from leave, and she requested all the things I hadn't spoken up about." She got all of them. Bottom line: lobby for what you want!

If your company's breast-feeding policy—or physical space—is inadequate, familiarize yourself with your state's laws. I can't tell you how many horror stories I've heard about pumping facilities! I talked to a woman who had to pump in her office's kitchen, which didn't have a lock on the door. She backed her chair up against it to keep people from walking in on her. She had one colleague who would shove on the door, yelling, "The door is stuck again!" And she'd have to chirp, "No, I'm in here pumping!"

One woman I talked to worked in an office with an open floor plan, and she had no alternative but to pump in her office restroom. She was disgusted by it. "You're essentially preparing your child's lunch in a public bathroom," she said. She befriended a company a few floors up, and they let her use an empty office. When she'd get back to her desk, she'd often find a Post-it Note stuck to her computer monitor that read WHERE ARE YOU? Ultimately, she wound up sending an email to her boss whenever she left to go pump. "It was humiliating," she said.

And just as you have to walk the fine line between honesty and oversharing about family obligations, you need to also figure out whether (and when) to be forthright about pumping. "Sometimes you have to pop out in the middle of a conference," one woman told me. Without explanation, disappearing for thirty minutes can

PUMPING-AT-WORK BASICS

Ideally, before you go out on maternity leave, scope out the space your office has allocated for pumping mothers, and look for the things on this list.

- A private enclosed space with a locking door (any windows should have shades or opaque glass).
- A built-in sign that can be adjusted to read that the room is either in use or available. (Trust me: this will be taken much more seriously than will a taped-up handmade sign.)
- A conveniently placed electrical outlet.
- A comfortable chair.
- Easy access to a sink, microwave, and refrigerator. (Ideally, these things will be actually in the room! If not, see if your employer will buy a mini fridge and compact microwave that you can use for sterilizing parts.)
- A scheduling system—if the room will be used by others. (Shared Outlook or Google calendars can be great for this.)
- Decent Wi-Fi reception and a phone line.
- A company-provided hospital-grade pump. (Though you should expect to bring your own pump parts, note that

look questionable, but if it's a large meeting, whom do you tell you'll need that time? "If you can't schedule a meeting for a certain time because you need to pump," she asked, "do you say it's because you need to pump? Or do you just *again* say you're unavailable?" She is torn because part of her thinks that it's important to normalize breastfeeding and pumping "and not let everyone pretend it doesn't exist," but she also recognizes that it's sometimes just too much information.

One of my friends came up with a code statement that she used with her direct report: "I have to do a thing." They never explicitly discussed it being about pumping, but her direct report understood. I

some companies will purchase the pump parts for new moms, so be sure to ask.)
- A mirror, so you can check your appearance (no visible spills!) before leaving.

Some other nice-to-haves in that space:

- A basket or box of disposable nursing pads.
- A wet-wipes dispenser, or paper towels and cleaning solution for any spills.
- Cubbies or drawers where women can leave their pumps and other equipment.
- A water cooler or water pitcher.
- Healthy snacks (for low-blood sugar pumping sessions).

If there's something on this list that isn't there, *ask for it.* Your company has no way to know what you need unless you tell them. Some of these are "luxuries," but all of them will make your day-to-day life easier, which will make your work life more productive.

regularly pumped while on conference calls, and more than once I was asked if I was sitting next to the copy machine; the others could hear the wheezing, whirring noise of the pump through the phone.

You may find support in the most unexpected places. Lynn Perkins did, on a business trip with her younger, male, childless boss. When she landed in Los Angeles she realized she'd left her pump on the TSA scanner—in San Francisco. Panicked, she told her boss what had happened, and he sprang into action. "What do we need to do? Can we find a Babies"R"Us?" It turned out his dad was a pediatrician, and he approached it as their problem, not hers.

It's one thing to pump in your office; it's considerably more fraught to figure out how and where to pump in a client's office. One woman who works at advertising firm Ogilvy & Mather told me, "It was my first time meeting a new client, and I felt embarrassed to ask if they had a place to pump." Instead, she pumped quickly in the bathroom and poured the milk down the drain because she wouldn't be able to keep it cold. "I felt bad that I wasn't more assertive, but it just felt so awkward for me to have that conversation."

But take heart: some companies have become really thoughtful and proactive about nursing mothers. IBM announced in 2015 that they'll ship breast milk home for new mothers who are traveling; it's a small cost to them, but can make a huge impact on their employees.

PUMPING-AT-WORK LIKE A PRO

"There's a paddling under the surface that you don't want to bring up," one pumping mom told me, "but it is so lonely to feel like you're doing it alone." But I promise you: you're not. Here are the best tips I heard from other women in your shoes:

DOUBLE UP ON PUMP PARTS. Instead of cleaning everything between sessions, you can bring home two or three sets of flanges and bottles and throw them in your dishwasher overnight.

CONSIDER DOUBLING UP ON PUMPS. Lugging a pump to and fro every day makes it hard to feel like anything but a milk machine. If you're pumping at home as well, borrow the base unit from a friend who is no longer pumping or buy yourself a second pump. Alternately, if there are other nursing moms, see if any want to split the cost of renting a hospital-grade pump.

PUT *EVERYTHING* IN THE FRIDGE. You can get away with skipping washing up if you put your flanges and other pump parts in the fridge between sessions. One mom told me that she bought a mini fridge for her office so she could easily store pump parts there.

PICK UP SOME MICROWAVABLE STEAM BAGS. You put all of your parts in, add two ounces of water, seal the bag, and microwave it for three minutes. (Try the Medela brand or the ones that Dr. Brown's sells.)

BUY A HANDS-FREE PUMPING BRA. One mom on weeSpring.com wrote, "If you think you don't need one of these, try sitting for fifteen minutes with your hands on your boobs."

WEAR A NURSING COVER WHILE YOU PUMP, IN CASE YOU ARE WALKED IN ON. If you're in a locked room, this is less of an issue, but I've heard some horrible stories about unwelcome walk-ins. It's still awkward, but you're at least preserving a little modesty.

BE PREPARED FOR SOME SERIOUS SPILLS AND LEAKS. Keep wet wipes, extra nursing pads, and a large Ziploc bag in your pumping bag or desk. Keep a whole extra *outfit* at work as an insurance policy. (It's like an umbrella: if you have it, you'll never need it.)

BLOCK OUT TIME IN YOUR CALENDAR NOW FOR PUMPING. Set recurring calendar items for every day, two or three times a day. You can always adjust them, but this way you can aim to schedule your day around your pumping, rather than fitting pumping into your day.

CHOOSE PUMPING-FRIENDLY CLOTHING THAT DOESN'T REQUIRE YOU TO STRIP HALF-NAKED. That means button-down shirts rather than sheath dresses. Anything designed for nursing also offers easy access for pumping.

→

IF YOUR COMMUTE INCLUDES A LONG CAR RIDE, CONSIDER PUMPING WHILE DRIVING. You can buy a car adapter for your pump, and with a hands-free bra and a nursing cover over it, no one would know you're pumping.

PLAN AHEAD FOR CLIENT MEETINGS OR ANYTHING ELSE THAT WILL BRING YOU OFF-SITE. Ask in advance if they have space where you can pump. Send an email to someone there that you feel comfortable with, explaining that you have a new baby and will need some space to pump. If they don't have a designated pumping space already, they'll appreciate the advance notice so they won't have to scramble when you show up.

IF YOU'RE TRAVELING, USE A THERMOS OR OTHER INSULATED STAINLESS-STEEL BOTTLE TO TRANSPORT COLD MILK HOME. As long as the milk is already cold when you transfer it to the Thermos, it'll stay cold for up to twenty-four hours. I transported a gallon of milk home on an airplane in two "beer growler" Hydro Flasks. It's a lot easier than messing with ice and a cooler.

IF YOU'RE STAYING IN A HOTEL, CALL AHEAD OF TIME. Ask if you can have a small fridge with a freezer in your room; if you get any push-back, tell them it is for medical liquids. Also ask if you can store something in their restaurant kitchen freezer, in case the in-room freezer is lukewarm (which it will be, 50 percent of the time). One woman told me she wound up with a room upgrade when she requested a fridge!

IF YOU'RE PUMPING IN AN AIRPORT, some airline lounges will have a front area with semi-private chairs where people presumably make Very Important Phone Calls. Even if they won't let you in to the full club if you're not a member, they will likely let you use this little front area.

You could fill a book with guidance on pumping when you go back to work—and one very savvy, smart mother published one recently. Jessica Shortall is the former director of giving for TOMS shoes and the author of *Work. Pump. Repeat.—The New Mom's Survival Guide to Breastfeeding and Going Back to Work.* It's a fun, quick, insightful read, rife with hands-on advice about everything from assembling your pump to what you'll need to pump on an airplane.

BABY BRAIN IS REAL, BUT IT'S NOT WHAT YOU THINK

No matter what words someone uses to describe it, I bristle when I hear the words "baby brain" or "mommy brain" or "pregnancy brain." There's an apology implicit in those terms, as though it's a weakness to experience some neurological changes while *growing a human being* inside your body. I heard about a psychology professor who called it "placenta brain"; at least with that phrasing you're not blaming the mother or the infant. But the truth is, all of those terms hurt women, because they undermine our perceived capacity to continue to think straight when we have a child. "If you're caring for a sick parent, no one will say you have sick-parent brain," one executive told me. "Yet you're probably considerably more distracted."

In her book *The Female Brain* (a fascinating read for pregnant and new moms), Dr. Louann Brizendine writes that it all really comes down to evolution. The physical cues (growing a fetus, giving birth, nursing a newborn) trigger new neurochemical pathways, which result in a "motivated, highly attentive, and aggressively protective brain that forces that new mother to alter her responses and priorities in life."[11] But a shift in priorities doesn't mean less cognitive capacity.

In 2014, psychiatrist and researcher Dr. Laura J. Miller, medical director of Women's Mental Health at Edward Hines Jr. VA Hospital, published a review of the literature to date on cognitive and emotional changes during pregnancy and the postpartum period. She explains that almost every study found subjective impairments of both memory and attention, but *subjective* is the operative word there. Though pregnant and postpartum women report having less mental capacity, when they're tested in a lab alongside nonpregnant women, there's no significant difference in performance. In considering their findings, Dr. Miller and other scientists have theorized that when pregnant women and new mothers have *normal* cognitive slips, they overattribute them to their "mommy brain," having internalized this pervasive cultural assumption.

Losing focus around 3:00 or 4:00 PM is such a prevalent phenomenon that journalists and scientists coined a term to describe it: the midafternoon slump. Studies have shown that a thirty- to sixty-minute nap can radically boost productivity. Yet when women feel unproductive or ineffective late in the day, they often internalize it as a failing. "I lost the last 15 percent of my day once I got pregnant," one woman told me. "I could push through on adrenaline until 4:00 PM, but after that, I couldn't even write an email."

Michael Silverman is a licensed psychologist and clinical neuroscientist who has conducted extensive research on the neurobiology of mood change during pregnancy and following childbirth. He performed a study in his lab that reinforces this gap between perceived performance and *actual* performance; he sees this play out in his clinical practice as well. "Women report that they have a worse memory and are unable to concentrate," he explained, "but when we test them, they don't show it." In other words, the notion of "mommy brain" can be a self-fulfilling prophecy. "If you feel like you're doing poorly, it's going to play with your mood," which then *actually* impacts your performance.

In Dr. Miller's findings, there were two instances in which there *was* a meaningful difference in performance: when the memory tasks required "effortful processing" (like rehearsing a speech to remember it), or when a "naturalistic" task like remembering to call the lab at a certain time following the study. In both of those instances, simple crutches can level out the playing field, and sometimes just being aware of the challenge can mitigate it. Many if not most of us use these crutches regularly: setting calendar reminders, maintaining checklists, and taking detailed notes—anything to essentially "back up" the pressing information stored in our brains.

One woman told me she feels she's lost her short-term memory, and reluctantly admitted she has to write anything down if she's to have any hope of recalling it later. "I don't know anyone's name," she said, "especially out of context." She relies on Post-it Notes for reminders. Some of this comes down to the multitasking exercise I discussed earlier: when you have a child, you're just *busier*. You're cramming more into your day; you have more to remember. Busy people need more strategies for keeping track of everything. "It's why executives have executive assistants," one mom wryly observed.

The memory challenges that have surfaced in scientific research are entirely surmountable—and they're not permanent. "My partners ribbed me about coming back and being less sharp," one investor told me. "I was so angry about that that I was determined not to be." She admitted to herself that she had slower recall sometimes, but "that's just because I was exhausted."

It's not just about the "tough" stuff, like remembering what was discussed in a meeting. They'll set calendar reminders even for little household tasks like taking the clothes out of the dryer. I use a daily alarm on my iPhone to remind me to pick up my son from preschool, because without it, I'd lose track of time and forget. One new mother told me, "My wife would ask me to do something little around the house, and I'd forget five minutes later that she'd asked." The fact that her wife's memory was intact made these lapses even more frustrating—for both of them.

It's easy to feel, when you can't remember basic words like "Kleenex," that your brain is broken, and you're never going to regain the cognitive capacity you had before you had a baby. But you will: nothing has changed in your brain that diminishes your intelligence.

Your attention to detail may have slipped, but you can get that back—if you want it.

I was always meticulous in my office, the one who'd catch little errors and never let anything slip through the cracks. After my son was born I started a new job, and my boss (the professional equivalent of a Tiger Mom) would frequently point out typos in the documents I was delivering to her. Even after I'd proofread something, there would still be a mistake or two, and I was totally despondent. In hindsight it sounds so silly, but in that moment I was certain I'd peaked professionally before my baby was born—and I was now destined to do shoddy work for the next twenty years.

It's been almost four years now, and I still haven't gotten better about the little details. But I've realized that, in part, it's because I don't *want* to be nose-down in the minutiae anymore: I want to be thinking about big-picture strategy. And that's a better use of my time anyway. My professional capacity isn't lower, it's just *different*. I can live with that.

SLEEP DEPRIVATION

As mentioned above, "mommy brain" is greatly influenced by sleep deprivation, the effects of which extend well past just feeling sluggish. Other impacts: your body's ability to ward off infection and viruses is weakened, your concentration and mood are decreased, your ability to learn and consolidate memories is diminished, and your reaction times are slower. Plus, if you're chronically overtired, your body's adrenaline and cortisol are chronically elevated. Those hormones create a heightened sense of stress that make it hard to function, both physically and emotionally.

Hawley Montgomery-Downs is a professor who runs the Sleep and Sleep Disorders Laboratory at West Virginia University; she is also a mother of three. She's conducted extensive studies monitoring the sleep patterns of postpartum women. But she's limited in the lab-based research she can do on REM sleep disruption. "It's just not ethical," she said, to deprive subjects of REM sleep. "Yet millions of women are exposed to it."

And though we talk a lot about sleep deprivation, in real terms what most new mothers experience is sleep *fragmentation*. Added up, the blocks of time these mothers do sleep often reach the seven-and-a-half-hour threshold that's considered "enough" sleep, but those hours are rarely contiguous. Dr. Montgomery-Downs explained that we cycle through sleep in ninety-minute increments. "If one of those cycles gets interrupted, it's not like a book where you can put it down and pick back up where you left off. You have to start over."

The real problem, in her words, is that "the best chapter is at the end, because that's when REM sleep is happening. Every time your baby cries, or even sighs in a funny way on the baby monitor, you wake up and aren't getting to that REM."

In her research, funded by the National Institutes of Health, Dr. Montgomery-Downs tracked women in the three months after childbirth, equipping them with a monitor for tracking their sleep and an electronic game for testing their reaction time every morning after waking up. One week after their babies were born, their results matched those of the control group, but as more time passed their reaction times got slower and slower, until they were poorer than they'd be if they were legally intoxicated.

Even when the women were back to a "normal" amount of sleep, they had accrued an enormous sleep deficit, and still experienced sleep fragmentation to boot. Two years later, tests showed some lingering impairment. So "get more sleep" isn't a cure-all, because they're already getting enough. "You've chopped your sleep up into confetti and scattered it everywhere," Dr. Montgomery-Downs explained. The trick is piecing it back together so that you get enough *consecutive* sleep cycles to afford you the restorative REM you need.

While it's depressing to think about years of interrupted sleep, I personally found Dr. Montgomery-Downs's research validating. It helps me understand why I'm still a little foggy even though my

SLEEP TRAINING

Some parenting guides tout sleep-training "cry it out" methods like the Ferber method. Such approaches are incredibly controversial, and nasty, spiteful comments break out on message boards whenever the issue of sleep training comes up. I'm not weighing in on this debate except to say that I heard from a number of women that sleep training was the key to their sanity and success in returning to the office.

One woman even credited the continued success of her marriage to sleep training her children. "Every night," she told me, "we have from 7:00 PM to 9:00 PM together. We make a point of watching a movie together or lying on the couch and reading together." For women doing a "split shift," getting back on their computers at 8:00 PM, reliably getting their baby to sleep around 7:00 PM is critical to their ability to do their job.

Janet Krone Kennedy is the author of *The Good Sleeper: The Essential Guide to Sleep for Your Baby—and You*. She told me that many of the parents she works with struggle with early bedtimes. "It's heartbreaking at first," she said. "You feel deprived of time with your baby, and you worry that your kid is deprived of time with you. But babies need sleep," she continued, "and so do their parents."

Be realistic, though, about getting your child to sleep through the night by the time you go back to work. Dr. Kennedy explained that babies' biorhythms allow them to establish a reliable sleep schedule, and those biorhythms become more predictable when they're around three months old, as their bodies are finally producing enough of the hormones that regulate sleep and waking.

daughter has been sleeping through the night for six months. And even just being aware of having, in scientific terms, "mild cognitive impairment" can go a long way in combatting the psychological effects.

One of the especially tricky things about sleep fragmentation and REM deprivation is that you may not even be aware that you're impaired. This is another way that sleep deprivation mimics the effects of alcohol. Many of us have experienced that sensation that we're *fine* after a couple of drinks, until we hear our voices slurring or realize we're a little wobbly. What's different is that, when you've had a couple of glasses of wine, there's a clear cause and effect: you pour a glass of wine, you drink it, and you get a little loopy. With sleep fragmentation, you may not even remember the next day that you half woke a few times in the night three days out of the last week, so it's even harder to be mindful of it. "Assume that you *are* messed up," advised Dr. Montgomery-Downs. Just as with alcohol, we lose that personal insight and don't realize how impaired we are until we make a mistake.

"Knowing what to expect and understanding the consequences of sleep fragmentation will enable you to come up with a strategic plan," she explained. Turning over one bottle-feeding a night to your partner can enable you to get some back-to-back blocks of REM sleep. In my house, we stopped using a baby monitor, because every little noise would wake me up. (I realized quickly that if the baby was *really* awake and crying, I'd hear him through the wall.) Protecting your sleep is infinitely harder for single mothers who are on duty 24/7, but I know one single mom who has carved out one night every week when she sleeps through the night, because her baby's sleeping at his grandparents' house.

Michael Silverman used a "dimmer switch" analogy to explain the cognitive impacts of sleep deprivation. Imagine your brain as having tiers, starting with the brain stem that regulates your heart rate and breathing, reaching all the way up to the frontal cortex, which helps retain memories, drives decision-making, and enables you to speak fluently and meaningfully. As you turn up the knob on your dimmer switch, you slowly and progressively light up these tiers of the brain.

But when you're sleep-deprived, there isn't enough power to light your frontal cortex. "You need the light to come on all the way to have fully rational thought," Silverman explained, "but lack of sleep dims your frontal lobe." From a professional perspective, operating without the full capacity of your frontal cortex is going to make it hard to express yourself clearly or to remember the names of colleagues. You may struggle to stay focused, or you might find yourself unable to make simple decisions. When my daughter was six months old, I spent twenty minutes in the hand soap section of Target, paralyzed by the array of choices before me. Imagine the effects of that indecisiveness in your office, when you need to decide how to pitch a client or which bid to select.

Worse, sleep deprivation can be fuel on the fire of self-doubt. If you're forgetting colleagues' names or crippled by simple decisions, your internal dialogue may spin quickly out of control to thoughts like, *I've lost my touch*, or *I'm going to be fired*. And because your "dimmed" frontal cortex also keeps you from rationally considering your emotions, those negative thoughts play in your brain at a louder volume than the other things on your mind.

So, what can you do?

At the office, write things down. Remind yourself on paper (or on your computer or smartphone) that you need to send the report to the communications director by November 15. In meetings, more extensive note taking can be helpful for some, though when you're extremely exhausted it can be harder to process subtle cues about what's important and what's not—which means you simply write everything down. Silverman asked me, "Have you ever looked at notes you've taken under those conditions?" He likened them to music without tone. When it's especially important for you to pay attention to detail, consider recording meetings and conversations. Virtually all cell phones have this feature now, and it can be easily (and quietly) activated.

When possible, schedule meetings and calls for the times when you'll be most alert (most find mornings are best). If you're worried about careless mistakes, have someone check your work. If you find yourself zoned out and forgetting meetings or calls, set calendar alarms and set reminders on your phone. Put coping mechanisms in place, and don't feel ashamed about using them.

And most important: offer yourself a little self-compassion. This isn't just about being nice to yourself; according to Silverman, that self-compassion can halt that spiral of negativity.

POSTPARTUM DEPRESSION AND ANXIETY

One friend described her postpartum mood shifts to me as "feeling incredibly detached." She knew it wasn't clinical or pathological depression, but she still got fearful during these moments. She'd think to herself, *If something happened to my baby, I could go on. It would be okay.* And then she'd immediately feel terrible.

You don't know how prevalent those feelings are when you're in the thick of them because it takes an enormous amount of courage to talk about them. Who wants to be the mother who hasn't bonded with her child? But the truth is, those types of dissociative thoughts are in no way indicative of whether you love your baby. It's your brain grappling with this incredibly intense new relationship and this enormous new responsibility. One woman told me she finally recognized her postpartum depression when she realized she was drinking to excess at happy hours with her friends. She'd never had a drinking problem, and getting a cocktail after work was a casual, regular way she socialized. But after her son was born, she started relishing the escapism of a couple (or more) drinks.

Like almost anything, there's a spectrum to this. One woman picked up her iPad and was infuriated to find ten open tabs on Safari where her husband had Googled "postpartum depression." She felt like she was reacting normally to a big life transition, and meanwhile, her husband was trying to pigeonhole her into a diagnosis. A writer told me, "I was diagnosed with 'adjustment disorder' by my doctor. Who *doesn't* have a hard time adjusting to a new baby? We spend all of this time preparing for a new chapter that it becomes all-consuming and—by extension—incapacitating."

Scientists believe there are three components to prenatal and postpartum mental health: biological (your physiological response to hormonal changes), psychological (what your thought processes look like), and social (your support networks and community). If there's a significant disruption in any one of those areas, a woman is at risk of developing postpartum depression.

Those postpartum mood shifts don't always look like "typical" depression. One woman told me she was filled with blinding anger so severe she worried it would harm her relationships with colleagues. She had to get into the habit of waiting five minutes to respond to anything that rubbed her the wrong way so she could calm down and be rational. That anger makes some sense, in evolutionary terms: your maternal brain is fierce because, in cave-dweller terms, you need to protect your baby. Even without the threat of saber-toothed tigers, you react forcefully to anything that interferes with your ability to nurture your child (and that something can be as small as a colleague wasting your time).

"I constantly needed a plan," one woman told me. She had been through the whole new-mother thing twice already, but with her third baby she felt a crushing anxiety about being left alone with all three children. As a professional powerhouse who was used to juggling a hundred things at once, she was blinded by how overwhelming motherhood suddenly felt.

Postpartum anxiety can be as crippling as postpartum depression, but sometimes it's harder to identify and understand because the associated feelings are so foreign. One woman told me she spent her days at work gripped by fear that her baby would die, constantly wracked with terrible thoughts unless she got a periodic update from her nanny. Because you're so new to the whole parenthood thing, you might think those thoughts are normal and that everyone has them. And they *are* normal, and everyone *does* have them—but not necessarily to such an extreme. "They're advantageous and self-protective," Michael Silverman explained. "If you worry, *What if I drop my baby on the stairs?*, your next thought will be, *I'm going to hold the railing with one hand and the baby with another.*" But if such thoughts paralyze you throughout your day, they're not normal.

It's estimated that as many as 20 percent of women will experience some level of postpartum depression (PPD) or anxiety (PPA). But, though it's the most common complication from childbirth, many of the women I spoke with were never screened by their OB/GYN or their baby's pediatrician. That 20 percent number pales in comparison to the survey results I saw: 4 percent reported severe PPD or PPA, 15 percent reported moderate PPD or PPA, and 14 percent mild PPD or PPA. Another 22 percent said they weren't sure; it could have just been the baby blues. So that brings us to 55 percent of the two thousand women who responded.

Think about the impact of postpartum distress on the professional lives of women returning to work, spending their days beset by varying degrees of self-doubt and anxiety. In some extreme cases, women can barely get out of bed. According to the National Institute of Mental Health, depression annually costs employers $34 billion in lost productivity. At the individual level, though, depression— and the related loss of productivity—can cost women promotions, raises, even their jobs. Depression and anxiety can also fuel irrational thoughts about incompetence with work, with your child, or both. Small instances of self-doubt can easily snowball into fears like, *If I can't do this, then I must be bad at everything.*

The *good* news about PPD and PPA is that they are highly treatable, either through talk therapy or medication, or both. Yet only 31 percent of the women from my survey who experienced postpartum depression or anxiety got treatment: 12 percent took medication, 10 percent saw a therapist, and 9 percent did both.

Talk therapy helps women suffering from postpartum depression by rerouting some neural pathways. "Think of your neural pathways as a habit," one social worker told me. "We form them because at some point they serve us." Therapy helps people to create *new* habits and new ways of thinking.

She shared an analogy with me: your brain is a jungle, with tall grass and tangled vines. There's a path through it, but it's full of snakes. You're terrified of that path, but everything else seems impenetrable. Walking down that path feels like the only choice, even though the snakes keep biting you. In real life, that path is prompting scary thoughts like, *I'm never going to feel love for my baby*, or *What if I drown the baby while giving him his bath?*

"Therapy gives you a machete and some heavy boots to help you create a new path," the social worker explained. For women who've always strived for perfection, for instance, you might hack away at a path in which "good enough" is enough. It's hard work, and it's ongoing, because when you're feeling depleted and exhausted, you just want to put down the machete and walk down the path that's already clear. You have to deliberately steer that interior monologue away from the spirals of self-doubt and guilt.

Medication often helps because there's a real hormonal shift happening in your body in the weeks and months after giving birth. That said, we still don't understand much about *why* all of these things happen. During pregnancy, your estrogen levels spike to help promote growth in your baby.[12] After childbirth, those estrogen levels drop precipitously, and there's a theory that when estrogen plummets, it disrupts the body's ability to process serotonin, causing what's thought of as the baby blues. Research has shown that as many as 85 percent of women experience the baby blues, which manifests as tremendous emotional vulnerability. You're euphoric one minute, and you're a puddle on the kitchen floor the next. For most women, those serotonin levels normalize within a few weeks—but for some, they don't. Medications can help stabilize those hormonal changes and rebalance your brain chemistry.

DELAYED-ONSET DEPRESSION

When you think "postpartum depression," you might assume it's related to the first weeks and months after your baby is born, but we now know that mothers are at particular risk for the first twelve *months* after their babies are born.

For instance, weaning-related depression is another complicated facet of new motherhood that isn't talked about frequently enough. When my daughter was about eight months old, I'd dropped down to nursing her a couple of times a day and formula-feeding the rest of the time. Soon after, I got hit with horrendous migraines and had to take meds that were contraindicated when breast-feeding, so I stopped nursing, cold turkey. A week later, I couldn't get out of bed. I'd been tearful for a couple of days, but one morning I woke up paralyzed with despair. I told my husband I wasn't feeling well and slept in, but every time I tried to get up to shower, I'd break down into shoulder-shaking sobs and crawl back to bed, completely defeated.

My therapist later explained that, while we still don't know much about the underpinnings of the hormonal shifts that happen during weaning, there *is* a notable change in hormones. "Some women have a negative reaction to the depletion of certain hormones," he explained, "and others see problems from the surge in hormones." I rode it out, and within a couple of weeks I was functioning normally again—but in that first year of parenthood, weeks can feel like a lifetime. (If you want to read more about weaning-related depression, Joanna Goddard wrote a wonderful post about it, "The Hardest Two Months of My Life," on *A Cup of Jo*. It was a lifeline for me when I was struggling.)

Some other things that affect brain chemistry: sleep, nutrition, water, and oxygen. All of those things are disrupted for a new mom. You're up all night nurturing a baby. You're not eating healthy food and getting enough protein (the amino acids in protein play a role in neurotransmitters). The dehydration that results from breast-feeding is another stressor, as is not taking a deep breath since giving birth.

The transition back to work can reverse any strides you've made toward "normalcy" in the weeks and months after your baby was born. Those basic building blocks—getting sleep, eating nutritious food, drinking plenty of water, and regular deep breathing—are the foundation for both your mental health and your brain capacity.

If any of what you just read sounds familiar or resonates with you, tell your doctor, but also seek out support from a trained perinatal mental health professional. Finding an expert is important: there are alarming aspects of PPD that are actually quite "normal," and there are some run-of-the-mill depression symptoms that can be especially dangerous for women with PPD. Postpartum Support International (www.postpartum.net) has a national directory of counselors, with coordinators in each state to help you connect with a therapist who deeply understands the challenges of new parenthood.

MAKING TIME FOR YOU

I talked in the last chapter about how self-care is where the wheels come off the bus on maternity leave. This might be even more true once you go back to work. I asked every woman I talked to: "What do you do that's just for *you*?" More often than not, I heard silence, or a hesitant "I don't." A senior manager on Wall Street told me, "I always say that exercise is my alone time, but I never actually make it to the gym." A Yahoo executive confessed to being resentful that a pedicure was considered "her" time. One woman actually responded, "I laugh at the idea of time for myself! I daydream about being able to stay in bed with my coffee and a newspaper. It sounds totally ridiculous to people who don't have children."

A researcher at Kaiser Permanente, the health insurance provider, had an epiphany when she realized her stay-at-home mom friends were scheduling vacations for themselves and their husbands without their kids. "Meanwhile," she told me, "I'm feeling wracked with guilt because I want to go to the gym." Believe me: stay-at-home moms have earned a vacation from their jobs (taking care of their kids). But so have working moms, whether that's a week at a resort or an hour playing tennis a couple of times a week.

For the women who *did* carve out time that wasn't about either childcare or work, the common thread was that they locked it into their schedule well in advance. One had a regular Wednesday breakfast meeting with girlfriends; one of the reasons this worked was that setting social time in the morning meant it was less likely to get infringed upon by work. Another signed up for an eight-week mindfulness course on Monday nights. "I had no expectation about what I'd get out of it," she said, "except that it was a night that I didn't have to worry about feeding, bathing, or getting the baby to sleep." She loved the consistency of it. It was something she could look forward to and plan for. "The planning is as important psychologically as having the time itself."

Another woman has a regular routine with her husband: one night a week, she goes out with her friends (no baby, no husband); on another, he goes out with his. And once a week, they go out together. She sees that time as an investment in the success of their marriage, and on their dates they work hard not to sink into conversation about the logistics of their life or childcare.

"Getting time alone with my wife has been the hardest thing," one new mom told me. Many of the women I spoke with talked about consciously investing in their marriage, or they told me they regretted that they *hadn't*. "Spousal relationships tend to be pretty stellar when everyone is getting two hours of sleep," a consultant deadpanned. And there's always the maxim "A babysitter is cheaper than a divorce."

Morra Aarons-Mele told me, "I am pretty big on me time, but I had to overcome a lot of guilt to get there." She eventually realized that, if she wasn't happy, no one in her family would be. "I work really hard and save for things like therapeutic massage and acupuncture," she said. It's a stress release valve for her; she understands that, if she's frazzled and exhausted, she's going to be short-tempered with her kids.

When Lori Mihalich-Levin, a health care regulatory lawyer, returned to work after her second baby, she felt like "one plus one equaled eighty-five." She looked around and realized that no one else in her office was talking about this really difficult period. "You can take a class in hypnobirthing or how to give a newborn a bath, but there's no one teaching you how to hold on to your sanity when you return from maternity leave."

So she created an online class for pregnant women to help them have a calmer and more empowered return. "Your leave can be an asset to your career," she explained, "rather than a career-ender. Your mindset can impact your outcome." She also believes that "self-care is a muscle that you have to exercise." In her own life, that takes the form of a meditation practice—but in very manageable doses. She meditates with an app called Insight Timer five minutes a day, a few times a week. She carves out time from her commute for it: on a nice day, she stops on a bench between the metro stop and her office. If the weather is bad, she does the same thing in a hotel lobby. "It starts my day off on the right foot."

She also has a shower routine, which she calls "ISS": Intention, Stretch, Savor. She sets an intention (like going to bed at 10:00 PM, or remembering to smile if she's in a bad mood). She does a few yoga stretches to relieve some of the physical manifestations of tension, and then she stops to savor something that she appreciates, like a hot shower, or having a house to shower *in*.

Every night before going to bed, she jots down five things that she's grateful for in her gratitude journal. "It reorients going to sleep from, 'Oh my god, I have fifty thousand things to do,' to, 'I am really lucky.'"

The lesson in all of these practices: the small things can make a big difference. You don't have to overhaul your life; in fact, you probably can't. Be realistic about what you can fit in, and then stick to it.

WORTH REMEMBERING

- Use this time transitioning back to work to reset your work priorities. Be deliberate and thoughtful about how you use the (newly constrained) hours that you're in the office.
- Bring that same structure and introspection to your home life. Think about what's really *worth* spending time on.
- Stake your turf, both in terms of the work you want to do *and* the time in your day that you want to insulate from work.
- Be mindful about how you talk about your baby with colleagues. Really stop and think before you make baby-related small talk.
- Do whatever it takes to feel put together and confident about your appearance; this can mitigate the vulnerability you might feel while adjusting to life as a new mother.
- Keep building your stable of backup caregivers. (Yes, this is a recurring theme—intentionally so.)
- Pumping sucks. (Pun intended.) Make it suck less by arming yourself with best practices and other pro tips.
- If you're struggling, ask for help. Postpartum depression and anxiety are the most common side effects of childbirth; fortunately, both are highly treatable. It is *not* all in your head.
- Consciously invest in *you* time. As the song goes, "If mama ain't happy, ain't nobody happy."

PART 3.
PAYING IT FORWARD

CHAPTER 8

WHAT TO DO TO DRIVE CHANGE

C hrysula Winegar, the founder of Wake Up World Communications, has led countless successful campaigns for social change. She believes, "When you wake up a mother, you wake up the world."

"Noise *matters*," she said. "Attention matters, media matters. Governments and companies pay attention when the rallying cry gets loud enough." And there are lots of ways to be noisy without jeopardizing your job.

You wouldn't be reading this book if you weren't a do-er, so here are some things you can do to make a meaningful impact. And if you're in a position to influence your company culture, you'll also find ways to move the needle organizationally.

WHAT YOU CAN DO
Speak Up About What You Want, and Why You Want It

One of the women I interviewed works at a major nonprofit that focuses on women's issues, yet they only afforded six weeks of paid leave to their employees. "We talk about our work and the impact it has on women globally," she said. "But we don't personify the values we espouse." (Note: though they were generous by U.S. standards, they were paltry compared to most developed countries.) But when a high-profile executive got pregnant, the organization overhauled the policy. It turned out that the senior team *had no idea* how weak their own policy was.

Don't expect that your company or manager will anticipate your needs—or is even paying attention. Ask for what you want, and explain why you think it's best for the *business*. (In the case of this nonprofit, it would have been a PR nightmare if it had leaked that their family leave was so stingy.) And this applies not just to leave, but also to flexibility when you return.

Vote with Your Feet

We've talked about being cautious about asking too many family-related questions in the job interview process. But, once you have an offer letter, open the floodgates. Get the nitty-gritty details of their parental-leave policy, ask how they manage reentry for women returning from leave, and ask for an introduction to women working there who have young kids.

If you're declining a job offer, and their policy is weak or the culture seems unfriendly to working mothers, tell them that. It doesn't have to be the *primary* reason, or even the secondary reason, but make sure they know that they've lost a candidate that they wanted to hire in part because they don't have adequate supports for working mothers (and fathers).

Use Exit Interviews as a
Soapbox for Better Family Policy

You can't always be a crusader, but one low-stakes (yet high-impact!) opportunity to make your voice heard is your exit interview. You've already moved on: you don't have to worry about getting stigmatized at the company. If their parental-leave policy isn't outright *phenomenal*, tell your interviewer that was one of your deciding factors in leaving. Cite the policy, your company culture, the industry culture—even all three.

It is costly for them to replace you, far more costly than covering sixteen weeks of paid leave would have been. Help them draw a straight line between their policy toward parents and their employee retention.

In speaking up, you are doing more than just paying it forward for the other women in your company. Remember that a rising tide floats all boats. I heard of one old-school tech company in the San Francisco Bay Area that had to overhaul their stingy two weeks of maternity leave because the Facebooks and Googles of the world were grabbing all the top talent; you could be instrumental in driving change like that in your whole industry.

Join an Advocacy Organization That's Fighting for Workplace Equality

Grassroots activism works. But I'm also going to be realistic here and assume that, as a working mom (or soon-to-be mom), you have limited community organizing time. So add your voice to an organization that's already laid the groundwork, like MomsRising or A Better Balance. At www.momsrising.org you can find a list of all the pertinent federal legislation that's coming down the pike—and add your signature to their petitions. A Better Balance has similar "hot buttons" that allow you to support meaningful legislation.

Reach Out to Your Representatives in Government

I worked in politics for most of my twenties, and I can tell you with absolute certainty: it is elected officials' *job* to listen to you. They're called "representatives" for a reason: to represent you and make sure your voice is heard. Chrysula Winegar told me, "Most women just don't understand the power they wield as constituents. Your elected officials work for *you*."

Send an email to your representatives' offices. While you might wonder what your one effort can do, correspondence like that matters; often elected officials count the number of communications they receive on a particular issue. So take the time to pick up the phone: ask to speak to the official's legislative director, find out exactly where your representative stands, and share your perspective.

And think local as well as national. The most progressive policies to date have come at the state level. As of 2015, California, New Jersey, and Rhode Island afford paid leave, and other states have legislation pending.

WHAT COMPANIES CAN DO
Focus on *Family* Leave, not Maternity Leave

Cynthia Calvert, president of Workforce 21C and a senior advisor to the Center for WorkLife Law, believes that we'll start to see the tide turning for mothers as more employees care for aging parents—a situation that can ultimately be much more long-term than pregnancy.

In the meantime, though, *stop calling it "maternity leave."* Dads have family responsibilities too. Give them some paid time off—and not just a week. Sex discrimination laws require that fathers get the same amount of baby-bonding time as mothers. If you already have a paternity leave policy, encourage your employees to use it (many don't!) by being transparent about the percentage of dads or nongestational moms who took advantage of it. Aim for 100 percent.

Replace every reference to "maternity leave" with "parental leave" in your literature and communications—and make sure all employees, especially managers, are aware of that change. Culturally, a semantic shift like that can go a long way.

Make "Inclusion" a Mantra, and Go Beyond Just Policy

Having a generous family leave policy is just a building block; you need to invest in culture to make a real difference.

I talked to the chief diversity officer of a Fortune 500 company that has a particularly strong reputation for being family-friendly. I asked how they conveyed that value all the way down the line, through all of their managers. She talked about inclusion: "Diversity only gets you so far. You need to ensure your employees are thriving. Everyone has to feel like they can be heard, and they also need to feel everyone can be successful."

To that end they emphasize—and reemphasize—inclusiveness as a company value. Managers are rated not just on their accomplishments, but also on how they've achieved those accomplishments. Their direct reports rate them on how supportive and flexible they are, and the company holds leaders accountable to those standards.

So when you're talking about flexibility, explain how it applies to everyone in the company. Vocalize that teleworking or the ability to shift hours applies as much to the twentysomething grad student taking evening classes, as to the thirtysomething whose mental presence depends on going to yoga twice a week, or the fortysomething who coaches his niece's basketball team on Tuesdays after school.

Prioritize Quality over Quantity

Even before she had a baby, Katie Duffy would leave her job at Democracy Prep Public Schools at 6:00 PM because she wanted to have dinner at home with her husband. When she caught derisive stares from some of her colleagues, she stood up for herself, telling them: "Just because you're here at 10:00 PM doesn't mean that you're doing more than me."

When she became CEO, she told her team, "You won't win points from me by standing still long enough that everyone else leaves."

In too many companies, it's presumed that the people who are working longest are the ones working hardest. So break down that culture, not just for the parents but for all employees.

THE GOLD STANDARD IN PAID PARENTAL LEAVE

Over the year I've spent working on this book I've marveled at the steady stream of press releases from multinational companies vaunting their innovations in making families feel more welcome in the workplace. Netflix announced unlimited paid leave, and Amazon announced their "leave sharing" policy, which allows an Amazon employee's spouse to partake of their newly generous benefits. Even old-school companies like Nestlé muscled in on the action, announcing they were doubling their paid maternity leave. It almost feels like we're embarking on an arms race of generosity to new parents, and I am overjoyed to witness it.

Here are a few of my favorite policies:

VODAFONE: In 2015, the telecom giant announced that, in addition to affording all new mothers sixteen weeks of fully paid leave, they offer an additional six months in which mothers receive 100 percent of their salary for thirty hours a week of work.

GOOGLE: Susan Wojcicki, the CEO of YouTube, was the sixteenth employee at Google, and took the job while she was pregnant with her first child. She is widely credited with being the driver behind Google's eighteen weeks of paid leave—a policy that resulted in a huge jump in employee retention, with 50 percent more new parents returning to work after leave. (So, for 12.5 percent more of an employee's annual salary, Google retained 50 percent more employees.)

FACEBOOK: It shouldn't come as a surprise that the company Sheryl Sandberg helps lead has a policy generous to both new moms and new dads. After all, if women are going to lean in, they need their partners to be *true* partners in their family's care. (Notably and laudably, this policy was in place even before

Sandberg got there.) And a literal bonus: Facebook's seventeen weeks of leave also comes with $4,000 to help defray the costs of having a new baby.

CHANGE.ORG: Generous policy isn't just for supersized companies and tech titans. With about three hundred employees in eighteen countries, Change.org set their global leave policy at eighteen weeks for all parents.

BLACKSTONE GROUP: In April 2015, the Blackstone Group, a leading private equity firm, increased their leave for new mothers from twelve weeks to sixteen weeks. They saw it as an opportunity to take a leadership position in an industry that has historically struggled to attract women. (Not long after that announcement, rival firm Kohlberg Kravis Roberts announced a policy that got shorthanded as "flying nannies": they'll pay for a caregiver to tag along on a business trip, so a new mother can bring her baby.)

Wear Your Parental-Leave Policy on Your Sleeve, and Make Family a Narrative

Post your parental-leave policy on the "Jobs" page of your website. Be thorough: explain exactly what it means, without vagaries. Specify how long you need to work at the company to be eligible for paid leave, exactly how many weeks you're entitled to, and what percentage of your salary you'll receive during that time. If your company allows flexibility in how an employee takes that time, explain how that works. If you have state-of-the-art pumping rooms, trumpet that—or build them if you don't.

When you're interviewing employees, proactively bring up your family policy. Christine Anderson, the managing director of global public affairs at Blackstone, told me that when she interviews female candidates she speaks up about work-life balance. "I don't know if any of this is on your mind," she'll say, "but these are questions I never felt like I could ask when I was interviewing." She then talks about how she's had four children while working there, and how it's been possible.

Put Your Money Where Your Mouth Is

One major investment company—a company whose mission (and profit!) is centered on personal investing—*double-matches* the first 10 percent of salary that you put into a retirement account. That's a shining example of putting values into practice: they care about the future financial health of their employees, so they put significant funds toward encouraging them to save.

Ironically, they offer only forty-two days of paid maternity leave, which can shake a family's financial health. In the broad context of American companies, this policy is generous, but if a woman wants to take the full amount of leave she's entitled to under the FMLA, she's looking at a month without a salary. So while this company invests in their employees' long-term financial health, they jeopardize it in the short term.

If your company professes to care about its employees, allow them to become parents without having to choose between paying their mortgage and taking twelve weeks to bond with their newborn. As one CEO told me: "Generosity brings loyalty."

This is still a huge sticking point for companies across the U.S. In my survey, only 56 percent of women I interviewed received more than two weeks of paid time off when they had a baby. And while many companies argue that they can't afford it, the truth is that the cost of a fully paid maternity leave equates to a 25 percent retention or hiring bonus.

Jennifer Dulski told me of Change.org: "We're in the business of positive social change. It was natural for us to think about how to help employees." But when they implemented 18 weeks of paid leave for all parents, they didn't think about just the touchy-feely aspects:

they looked at the numbers. "We did extensive cost-benefit analysis." In addition to seeing that the cost of coverage for new mothers didn't make a dent in their organizational budget, they've found since that morale has soared. "My wife works for the government," one new father told me. "I got three times as much paid leave as she did. Why would I ever leave this company?"

When considering what your policy should be, don't ask, "What's average?" or, "What does everyone else do?" Don't strive for mediocrity; be exemplary. (And reap the PR benefits that come with that approach; do a Google search for "paid maternity leave" on any of the companies in the following sidebar to assess that PR impact.)

So, how can your company or organization get in on the PR bandwagon? Here are some ways you can walk your talk, in addition to offering twelve or sixteen weeks of paid leave.

- Make your employees "whole," filling in the gap between what disability covers and their salary.
- Allow flexibility in how they use their parental leave. Allow them to use it at any point in the twelve months following birth, so both parents can relay childcare to maximize the time one of them is home with the baby.
- Build in time for parents to ramp back up to full capacity— and give them the reins on their schedule (for example, allow them to come in late, leave early, or work four days a week).
- Offer a childcare stipend or "baby cash," as Facebook's $4,000 bonus has been called.

Use Objective Measures to See How Pregnant Women and Mothers of Young Children Are Faring

We've all heard the adage, "If you can't measure it, you can't manage it." Any company can call itself family-friendly (and genuinely believe it), but the hard, cold facts can tell a different story. Beneath the bromide of "this is a great place for women to work," metrics like new hires, promotions, compensation (both salaries and bonuses), voluntary and involuntary termination, and presence in the C-suite illuminate the actual reality—and how "family-friendly" that actually is.

Says employment lawyer Cynthia Calvert: "It's hard to be dismissive about your company's need to take action when you are looking at numbers that say no pregnant woman has ever been hired or promoted by your company." She explained that these types of statistics and numbers can help companies understand where they need to focus their efforts. If your pregnant employees are receiving smaller bonuses than their male counterparts are, for instance, you'll want to provide oversight on the compensation process to combat pregnancy bias.

Doing analysis like this on an annual basis will give you insight into whether you're making real progress.

Give Everyone Flexibility, Not Just Parents (or Executives)

Jennifer Dulski is the president and COO of Change.org. Under her leadership, the company upped their paid family leave to eighteen weeks at full salary, for *all* parents. But their family-friendly culture extends well beyond that. "Technology has mashed our lives together," Dulski told me. "You can't expect to have your employees live half of their lives at work and half of their lives at home." Because people are plugged in and connected through their smartphones in the evenings and on weekends, give them latitude to do the rest of their work when and where it fits into their lives.

That's not to say that spending time together as a team isn't critically important, but, as Dulski put it, "Don't demand face time as long as someone is doing their job really well."

THE HONEST TRUTH

From its first page, this book has been about not sugarcoating the realities of life as a working mother. So I'm not going to sugarcoat what it will take to really make a difference for women. I set out to give you a road map so that when you get to a sticky point or an obstacle that seems insurmountable—or you just want to throw in the towel—you have a reference point about how other women got past their hurdles. It's a personal guide and a playbook, and it's more about working within the system we've got than about radically overhauling it.

And that's because it's really, really hard for one individual to drive systemic change. You are or soon will be carrying enough weight just figuring out how to care for your new baby and keep your career on track. The day-to-day stuff is hard enough, and yet I'm asking you to think strategically about the year-to-year in your career—something so few people have the bandwidth for, never mind the people who are responsible for a tiny human. So I *know* you don't have time to be a revolutionary on top of all that.

But.

Our collective voice is *powerful*. We're seeing the very first ripple in what I believe is going to turn into groundswell change. Companies are starting to understand that, in order to compete for the best talent, they need to create a culture that welcomes working women. The dominoes are starting to fall, kicked off by innovators—in every sense of the word!—like Google and Facebook. "The next generation of employees *expects* flexibility," noted Dulski. So companies don't just need to make changes to retain women—they also need to make these changes to attract millennials.

On a legislative level, we're beginning to see a real focus on family life in the states. California led the charge in 2004, followed by New Jersey and Rhode Island. Many states have paid family leave legislation pending, and lawmakers are finally paying attention. Sending a letter to your legislator or signing a petition may feel like small steps, and I'm not going to lie to you: those *are* small steps. But tens of thousands of calls to a state's governor, and hundreds of thousands (or millions!) of signatures on a petition, capture the attention of the people who *are* in a position to be revolutionary, like Fortune 500 CEOs and state governors. I think about Hillary Clinton's moving speech when she dropped out of the presidential race in 2008: "Although we weren't able to shatter that highest, hardest glass ceiling this time, thanks to you, it's got about eighteen million cracks in it." Those individual votes and voices matter. You don't have to be the one who makes the glass rain down; just being one of those millions of cracks contributes to the change we want to effect.

We have come a long way, but our progress hasn't just been because of the big, press-worthy stuff like elections and Supreme Court cases. The day-to-day hustle of working women is driving that change too. Try to keep that in mind: even if it sometimes feels like what you're doing is going unappreciated or unnoticed, it's not. Trust me when I tell you that every working woman with young children appreciates the struggle and the effort you're putting in.

And as far as your efforts to get noticed go, every day that you put yourself out there as the rock star you are, you're poking a hole in someone's unconscious bias against mothers. They might not be aware of it—*you* might not be aware of it—but you're registering as someone who delivers, no matter the circumstance. You're breaking down bias when you hit your sales targets, when you land that important client, when you make that big presentation. When you earn that press accolade or win that competitive bid, you're also chipping away at the idea that mothers aren't as focused or engaged as nonparents. When you share an idea that's a game changer or finish a project that's challenged all of your colleagues, you're offering proof positive that whether or not you have a child isn't part of the equation that calculates professional success.

So keep doing what you do every day. Speak up for yourself. Build relationships, inside and outside your company and industry. Make every meeting count. Take on responsibility, even if you have to do it forcibly. Trumpet your accomplishments. Support the other women around you. Have a plan.

APPENDIX

PRACTICAL MATTERS

When I got pregnant with my son, I was working in wealth management, which meant I spent most of my days talking to people about their finances: their investments, their financial goals, their personal needs. A big part of my job concerned what's called "wealth planning." Wealth planning is a euphemism for estate planning, and it includes drafting a will and purchasing life insurance.

Now, I imagine that your own mortality is likely the *last* thing you want to think about when you're about to bring another human being into the world. Aside from all of the general busyness of pregnancy and newborn life, it is downright terrifying to acknowledge that you're not going to be around forever.

But because my day-to-day job involved so much thinking and talking about estate planning, talking to a lawyer about drafting a will and getting quotes for life insurance felt as routine to me as did finding a pediatrician. I consider myself lucky to have been immersed in these subjects, as I wasn't overwhelmed or intimidated by the choices I needed to make. There was no shroud of mystery around irrevocable trusts or powers of attorney, for example. I knew what I needed to do, and I did it.

That's my goal with this section: to pull off that shroud. I want to equip you with a basic understanding of the financial and legal nitty-gritty that'll ensure your family is provided for, even in the (remote! remote! remote!) event you or your spouse aren't able to do the providing.

Jane Barratt, who founded the women-focused investing startup GoldBean, told me, "Even the most type A prepared parents don't think beyond that first stage of financial impact. They think, *If we get a 529, we're all good.*" She advises that women (and parents in general) step back and think about the true financial impact of getting pregnant and having children. "Your baby is going to grow, no matter what you do," she said. "Spend some time getting yourself organized now."

She derided the idea, popular in personal finance circles, that you can save significant money by skipping your Starbucks latte every day. "It's about the big choices, like where you live and where you want to send your kids to school." She continued, "You're at a time in your life when you can make changes. Make some positive ones."

This sort of planning will enable you to continue with your career in the event something happens to your partner. But surprisingly, given the importance, these practical matters aren't really explained anywhere else. So much information and anxiety are foisted upon new parents, but basics like "you need to designate a guardian for your child" get lost in the shuffle. So, here's my quick-and-dirty guide to getting your affairs in order.

YOUR PRACTICAL MATTERS CHECKLIST

- Draft or update your will.
- Open a rainy day account and aim to put six months of living expenses in it.
- Purchase term life insurance.
- Compile all of your legal and financial information in one document and give it to a family member or trusted friend.
- Open a savings account for your child.

FIRST THINGS FIRST

If you don't already have a rainy day or emergency fund, start one. This comes before anything else, because it's your first line of defense should you find yourself not working for any stretch of time. A financial safety net is more important now than ever, but too few families have one in place.

Open a dedicated bank account, and divert a portion of your paycheck to it. Fill this pot *before* thinking about a down payment on a house or college savings.

Note: while conventional wisdom suggests you should reserve at least three months of living expenses, some financial planners recommend six.

BUDGETING FOR BABY

We've already covered that babies are *expensive*, particularly when it comes to childcare. For many families, childcare is the second biggest expense after their mortgage payment.

Have a conversation with your significant other about money earlier rather than later. Your paycheck is no longer just your paycheck, nor is your partner's. Are you going to pool your finances? Will you both direct deposit into one account, or will you maintain your own accounts and each contribute a set amount into a family expenses fund? Sorting out these details and putting vehicles in place early could spare you a lot of frustration down the road.

DRAFTING A WILL

A will isn't just about what happens to your assets; it puts forth your wishes about who will care for your children. But, as important as it is, of the more than two thousand women I interviewed for this book, only 20 percent had a will. "A will is an investment in your family's security," one lawyer told me. She also cautioned against online resources: "LegalZoom assumes everyone is cookie-cutter, but no one is." If you have a spouse who isn't a U.S. citizen, for instance, standard legal language from a form won't serve you. Plus, some states have very specific stipulations about how wills are to be signed; if your will doesn't meet all the requirements, it could be considered invalid.

When you draft your will, you can separately indicate a guardian, who would be responsible for the day-to-day care of your child, and a custodian, who would manage any assets you've left to your child. (If you already have a will, you'll want to review it to ensure you've designated the appropriate guardian.) Be sure to revisit your appointed guardian(s) from time to time to ensure they're (still) the right choice. You might set a calendar reminder for a check-in day every year, perhaps around your child's birthday.

There are two additional documents you'll want as well: a power of attorney and a healthcare proxy (also known as a living will).

Keep all these documents together in a secure, weatherproof, and fireproof place that your family is aware of. Consider too creating a summary document listing important contacts, savings or investment accounts, and the like.

LIFE INSURANCE 101

When you hear people talking about life insurance, they're usually talking about "term life insurance." It's called "term" because it's valid for a limited span of time, like twenty or thirty years. This type makes sense for families because its purpose is to ensure your children are provided for, so it expires around the time your children are adults and you no longer need it. (The insurance companies hope it expires before you do.)

When you're considering the length of the term you want to secure, keep in mind that, the older you get, the more expensive the monthly or annual payments will be. Buying a ten-year policy now may seem less expensive, but it will be costly to purchase a new policy when that one expires. (And there's no guarantee you'll still be insurable; if you were to develop a medical condition during those ten years, you may not find a company willing to take on your risk.) Because of this, the attorney I spoke with advised setting the term to coincide with your youngest child's college graduation.

The cost varies significantly based on your age and health. Note that you'll need to do some medical tests (blood, urine, etc.), and that your hormone levels during pregnancy and while breast-feeding may impact those tests. (As such, you might consider taking these tests before getting pregnant if you have that option.) If your agent tells you something in your results flagged you for a higher premium, send the results to your doctor to get her opinion.

As a rough ballpark, for a thirty-year-old woman in excellent health a twenty-year term policy costs $350 a year; a thirty-year term costs about $700 a year. For a thirty-five-year-old woman in excellent health, those policies cost about $100 more per year.

Other points to consider: life insurance is sometimes included in an employee benefits package. The coverage on those policies is typically low (around three times your annual salary). So do the actual math on what your family would need—including college expenses, day-to-day costs of living, and the cost of supplemental childcare—keeping in mind that, if you leave your job, your life insurance doesn't go with you.

One last thing: while many people are skittish about dealing with insurance agents or brokers, know that you can request a quote with no obligation to buy.

COLLEGE ACCOUNTS

A 529 account (named after section 529 of the tax code) is a tax-advantaged education savings account sponsored by states that allow funds to accrue without income tax. As some states include a tax deduction, the benefit to you as a consumer will differ on a case-by-case basis. The funds can *only* be used for educational purposes; if you wish to withdraw funds for another reason, you'll have to pay a 10 percent penalty and also pay taxes.

A 529 can be a great savings vehicle, but keep your own financial house in order. Don't save for a college account at the expense of saving for your retirement.

You can also open a UTMA (Uniform Transfers to Minors Act), which is a more flexible extension of a UGMA (Uniform Gifts to Minors Act).

FURTHER READING

If you're in the gobbling-up-information stage (when I was pregnant, I couldn't get enough!), these books offer practical, thoughtful, and in many cases *fascinating* perspectives on pregnancy, being a working woman, or both.

Babygate: How to Survive Pregnancy and Parenting in the Workplace
by Dina Bakst, Phoebe Taubman, and Elizabeth Gedmark

Written by three legal experts, this book goes into depth about your rights in the workplace and your employer's responsibilities to you. If you're concerned that you might be experiencing discrimination, you'll find state-by-state specifics on your legal protections.

Expecting Better: Why Conventional Pregnancy Wisdom
Is Wrong—and What You Really Need to Know
by Emily Oster

This is hands-down my favorite pregnancy book. The author is an economist who thought a lot of the pregnancy advice she was hearing (Do this! Not that!) sounded fishy. So she dove headfirst into the scientific papers and research, distilling what you really need to know during pregnancy. (Spoiler alert: sushi is okay, deli turkey is not.)

The Female Brain
by Louann Brizendine

Written by a neuropsychologist, this book is doubly enthralling: it covers all the changes that happen in a woman's brain as she becomes a mother, and it also sheds light on how a female infant's brain develops. (If you're having a boy, that's covered in *The Male Brain*—also a great read!)

The Good Sleeper: The Essential Guide to Sleep for Your Baby—and You
by Janet Krone Kennedy

This is a practical, actionable, informative guide to understanding infant sleep that's grounded in the science of how sleep impacts babies' development. The author, known as the "NYC Sleep Doctor," cuts through all the conflicting information out there and educates parents on the basics while also offering hands-on advice.

I Know How She Does It: How Successful Women Make the Most of Their Time
by Laura Vanderkam

Time-management expert Laura Vanderkam recruited more than a hundred superstar working women to keep detailed logs of their days to find out how they really "have it all." This book is a compilation of their best strategies, insights, and stories.

Origins: How the Nine Months Before Birth Shape the Rest of Our Lives
by Annie Murphy Paul

This is a cerebral and science-driven look—told through the lens of the author's own pregnancy—at what's going on in your body and how it impacts your child's life. It's a great read if you're experiencing a lot of wonderment about the idea of your body growing another body.

Overwhelmed: Work, Love, and Play When No One Has the Time
by Brigid Schulte

A single word sums up how most working mothers feel: "overwhelmed." And Brigid Schulte, a mother of two and a successful journalist, just *gets it*. An artful marriage of research and narrative, her book delves into the how and why of our American busyness while also tackling what you can do about it.

The Secret Thoughts of Successful Women: Why Capable People Suffer from the Impostor Syndrome and How to Thrive in Spite of It
by Valerie Young
This book was a revelation for me: countless successful women perpetually feel like a fraud, always fearing they're about to be "found out"—a malady so common it has a name. Young merges her academic perspective with compelling anecdotes from women suffering from impostor syndrome, including those of superstars like Kate Winslet and Maya Angelou.

Work. Pump. Repeat.: The New Mom's Survival
Guide to Breastfeeding and Going Back to Work
by Jessica Shortall
This is a reassuring, honest, and straightforward girlfriend-to-girlfriend guide to pumping in the office. Jessica Shortall covers everything from getting your pump out of the box to figuring out when it's time to wean—and she does so in a way that'll make you feel like a total champion.

WHAT YOU'LL FIND ONLINE

Talking to HR
- Questions to Ask HR About Parental Leave (printable worksheet)
- Checklist: Things to Do Before You Leave

Pregnancy Discrimination
- Where to Turn If You're Experiencing Discrimination

Making Your Partner a Partner
- Household Responsibilities Worksheet

Finding Childcare
- How to Write a Job Description for a Nanny
- Questions to Ask a Nanny
- Questions to Ask a Nanny's References
- How to Run a Background Check
- Sample Nanny Contract
- Questions to Ask a Daycare Facility
- Directory of Au Pair Agencies

Pumping at Work
- Pumping in the Office: What You'll Need
- Building up a Milk Store Before You Return to Work
- State Breast-Feeding Laws

NOTES

1. Elly-Ann Johansson, "The effect of own and spousal parental leave on earnings," Institute for Labour Market Policy Evalutaion, http://www.econstor.eu/bitstream/10419/45782/1/623752174.pdf.
2. Council of Economic Advisers, "The Economics of Paid and Unpaid Leave" (Washington, DC: The White House: Executive Office of the President of the United States, June 2014), www.whitehouse.gov/sites/default/files/docs/leave_report_final.pdf.
3. Karina Schumann and Michael Ross, "Why Women Apologize More Than Men: Gender Differences in Thresholds for Perceiving Offensive Behavior," *Psychological Science*, September 27, 2010, doi:10.1177/0956797610384150.
4. Louann Brizendine, *The Female Brain* (New York: Three Rivers Press, 2006), 99–100.
5. Adam Hajo and Adam D. Galinsky, "Enclothed Cognition," *Journal of Experimental Social Psychology* 48, no. 4 (2012): 918–925.
6. Broken down a bit more: of that one-third, the most common manifestation (39 percent) of discrimination was a reduction in responsibilities. Following that: 18 percent believe they weren't hired for a job because of their pregnancy or new baby; 11 percent saw their performance reviews impacted, even though they felt they performed just as well; and 10 percent were passed over for a promotion.
7. "Pregnancy Discrimination Charges FY 2010–FY 2014," U.S. Equal Employment Opportunity Commission, www.eeoc.gov/eeoc/statistics/enforcement/pregnancy_new.cfm.
8. Nicholas Bloom, "To Raise Productivity, Let More Employees Work from Home," *Harvard Business Review*, January–February 2014, https://hbr.org/2014/01/to-raise-productivity-let-more-employees-work-from-home.
9. Louise Nilsson, "Prolactin Reduces Fat Metabolism," University of Gothenburg: The Sahlgrenska Academy, March 31, 2009, http://sahlgrenska.gu.se/english/research/news-article//prolactin-reduces-fat-metabolism.cid876042.
10. Ibid.
11. Brizendine, *The Female Brain*, 96.
12. Harvard Mental Health Letter, "Beyond the 'Baby Blues,'" Harvard Health Publications, Harvard Medical School, September 1, 2011, www.health.harvard.edu/newsletter_article/beyond-the-baby-blues.

INDEX

ACKNOWLEDGMENTS

One of the unexpected benefits of writing this book was the opportunity to collect stories and advice from friends from every stage of my life, all of whom I always knew were smart and driven—but have blown me away with what they've accomplished professionally. Thank you to Jill Weiner Levine, Maryhope Howland Rutherford, Maurin Utz Scheetz, Alexandra Roberts, Sara Bowen Pratt, Julie Wall Williams, Sarah Culbertson Nau, Katherine McCleary, Jenny Cookson, Hilary Goodman Drake, Tracy Rahal, Ursula Cary Ziemba, Giovanna Gray Lockhart, Lee Dugger, Christine Anderson, Kay Moffett, Elizabeth Wills Chou, Selena Hsu, Margo Buchanan, Katie Duffy, Melissa Post, Jessica Solloway, and Amy Morrison. Laura Walsh Boone has been reading my first drafts since our freshman year of college, and her early edits were invaluable. Jaime Leifer and Rachel Rokicki shepherded this book from rough concept to final manuscript, and it's safe to say it wouldn't exist without them.

I owe a debt of gratitude to the women of The Li.st, who provided cheerleading for this book from day one—and were also a tremendous source of insights, anecdotes, and other sage advice on being a working mom. In particular: Morra Aarons-Mele, Jane Barratt, Naama Bloom, Sharon Feder, Fran Hauser, Jennifer Hill, Susan McPherson, Kristen Morrissey Thiede, Tereza Nemessanyi, Lacey Schwartz, Maria

Seidman, Cheryl Swirnow, Kathleen Warner, Margaret Wheeler Johnson, Chrysula Winegar, Cali Williams Yost, and—of course— the incomparable Rachel Sklar.

Thanks also to Mary Anderson, Emily Bassett, Lindsay Cookson, Stacey Delo, Susana Duarte, Jennifer Dulski, Cynthia Egan, Rachael Ellison, Erin Foust, Brittany Griffin, Valerie Grillo, Courtney Klein, Susan LaMotte, Kathy Liu Silverman, Caitlin MacGregor, Sara Mauskopf, Lori Mihalich-Levin, Jamie Mueller, Michelle Muller, Leslie Perdue, Kelly Prchal, Marisa Ricciardi, Jen Sargent, Andrea Sparrey, Kristen Stiles, Rachel ten Brink, Lucy Williams, Lana Zak, Katharine Zaleski, and Eve Zibel.

I leaned heavily on a panel of experts on everything from managing childcare to the effects of sleep deprivation: Lynn Perkins from UrbanSitter, Tom Breedlove from Care.com's HomePay, Vanessa Wauchope from Sensible Sitters, Julie Dye from Cultural Care, Brian Snearson, Ashley Normand, Zena Tamler, Pilyoung Kim, Michael Silverman, Janet Krone Kennedy, and Hawley Montgomery-Downs. Special thanks to Cynthia Calvert from Workforce 21C who reviewed (and re-reviewed) everything with a legal bent.

As they say, it takes a village—and while writing this book, I relied on an enormous village. *Thousands* of women from weeSpring.com contributed their experiences and perspectives, and I feel just plain lucky to be able to turn to a community so committed to helping support other parents and get back such a tremendous outpouring of wisdom.

And speaking of luck: I count myself incredibly fortunate to have a team of women supporting this book who just "got it" and believed in this book. Jennifer Carlson at the Dunow Carlson Lerner Agency was a champion for this idea, and I couldn't ask for a more encouraging or insightful editor than Laura Mazer at Seal Press. I'm grateful for Kirsten Janene-Nelson for helping shape the manuscript, from big-picture storytelling down to the smallest details, as well as to Donna Galassi and Eva Zimmerman for helping build an audience.

Most importantly, thank you to my family. My mom always made it look easy, and my stepdad embodied the mindset "make your partner a real partner" way before it was something people talked about. I won the husband lottery with Jack Downey, who not only encouraged me on a daily basis while writing this book, but also picked up miles of slack with both our children and our startup so I actually could *do* it. Thank you, thank you, thank you.

photo © Liliana Pena

ABOUT THE AUTHOR

Allyson Downey is an entrepreneur, writer, and parent who has built a career on the power of trusted advice. In 2013, she launched weeSpring, a Techstars-backed startup that helps new and expecting parents collect advice from their friends about what they need for their baby. weeSpring has received accolades from TechCrunch, Mashable, CNBC, and the *Daily Mail,* and it was heralded as "Yelp for baby products" by *InStyle* magazine.

Allyson has an MBA from Columbia Business School, an MFA from Columbia University's School of the Arts, and a BA from Colby College. She serves on the board of Democracy Prep Public Schools, one of the country's top charter management organizations, and lives in Boulder with her husband and two children. Visit her at HeresThePlanBook.com.

The Sh!t No One Tells You About Toddlers, by Dawn Dais. $16.00, 978-1-58005-589-5. In the second installment of her *The Sh!t No One Tells You* series, Dais offers real advice from real moms—along with hilarious anecdotes, clever tips, and the genuine encouragement every mom needs in order to survive the toddler years.

The Good Mother Myth: Redefining Motherhood to Fit Reality, edited by Avital Norman Nathman. $16, 978-1-58005-502-4. In an era of mommy blogs, Pinterest, and Facebook, *The Good Mother Myth* dismantles the social media-fed notion of what it means to be a «good mother.» This collection of essays takes a realistic look at motherhood and provides a platform for real voices and raw stories.

Motherhood and Feminism: Seal Studies, by Amber E. Kinser, $17, 978-1-58005-270-2. Part of the *Seal Studies* series, *Motherhood and Feminism* examines the role of feminism within motherhood—a topic that has garnered a lot of attention lately as society shifts to adapt to new definitions of these roles—and offers insight into the core questions of motherhood.

Running: A Love Story: 10 Years, 5 Marathons, and 1 Life Changing Sport, by Jen A. Miller. $17, 978-1-58005-610-6. Jen, a middle-of-the-pack but tenacious runner, hones her skill while navigating tricky relationships with men, relying on running to keep her steady in the hard times. As Jen pushes herself toward ever-greater challenges, she finds that running helps her walk away from the wrong men and learn to love herself while revealing focus, discipline, and confidence she didn't realize she had.

The Anti 9-to-5 Guide: Career Advice for Women Who Think Outside the Cube, by Michelle Goodman. $14.95, 978-1-58005-186-6. Many women would love to integrate their passion with their career and are seeking advice on how to do just that. Michelle Goodman has written a fun, reassuring, girlfriend-to-girlfriend guide on identifying your passion, transitioning out of that unfulfilling job, and doing it all in a smart, practical way.

FIND SEAL PRESS ONLINE

www.SealPress.com | www.Facebook.com/SealPress | Twitter: @SealPress